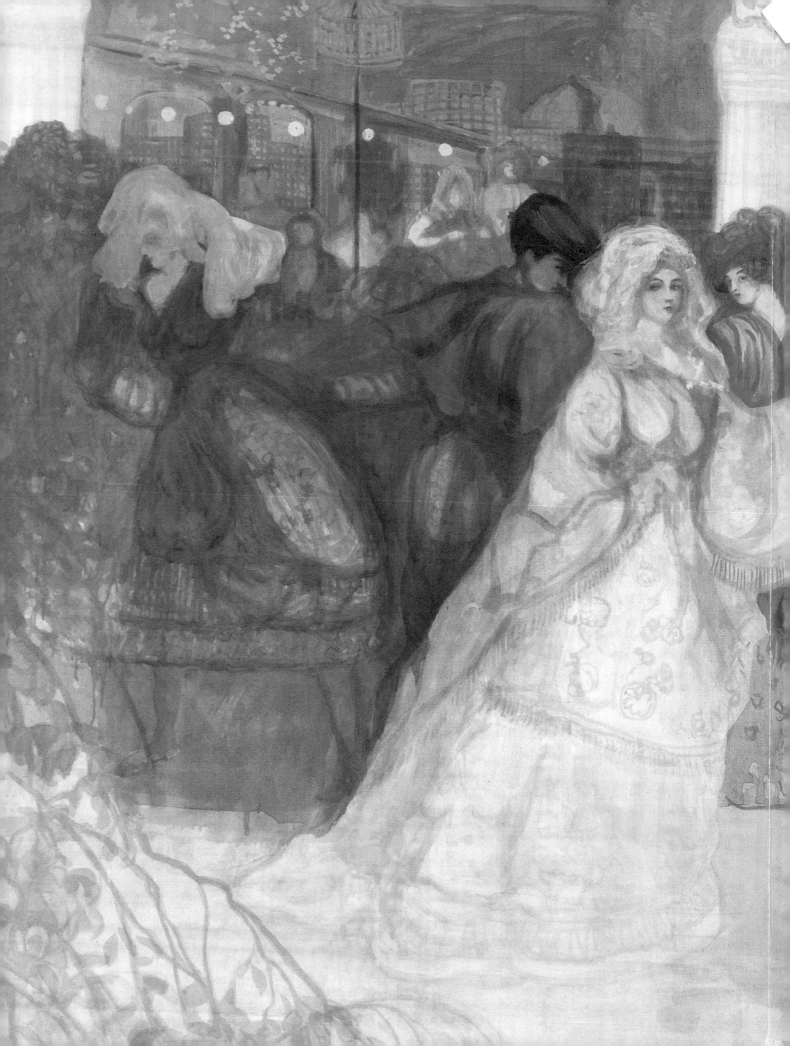

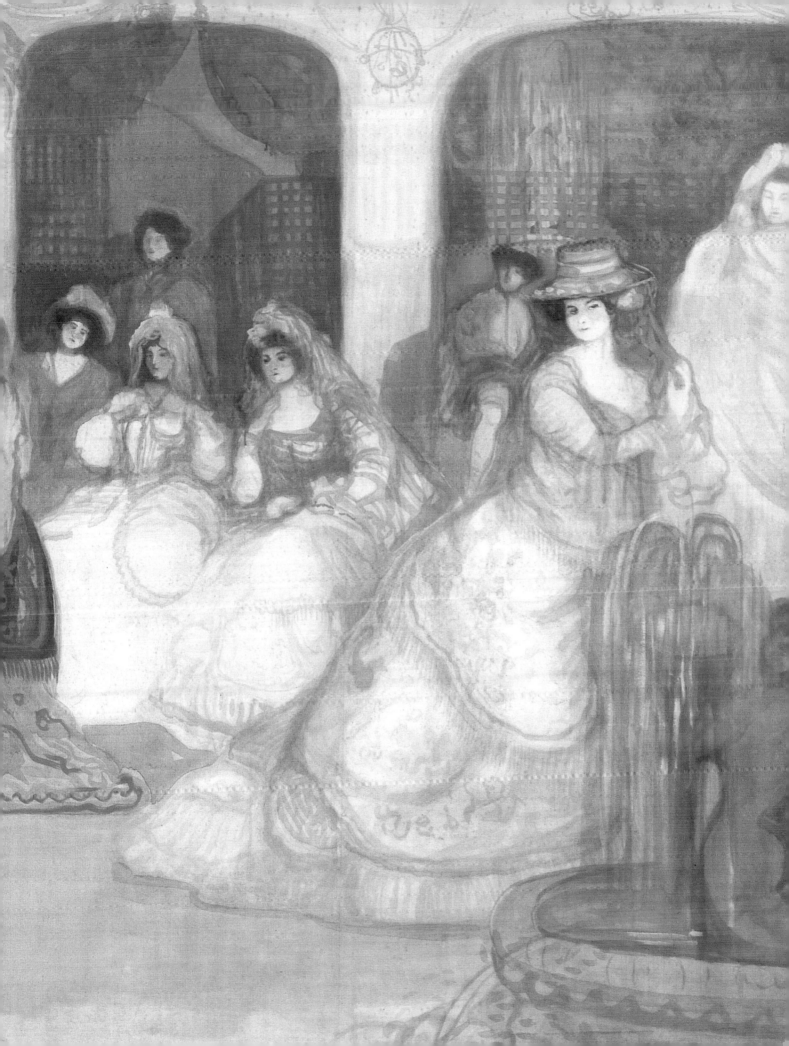

PAINTING ON SILK

STEP BY STEP ART SCHOOL
PAINTING ON SILK

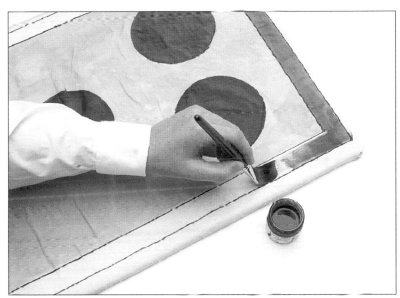

JANE WILDGOOSE

HAMLYN

First published in Great Britain in 1994
by Hamlyn an imprint of Reed Consumer Books Limited
Michelin House, 81 Fulham Road, London SW3 6RB
and Auckland, Melbourne, Singapore and Toronto

A CIP catalogue record for this book is available at the British Library

ISBN 0 600 58251 5

Produced, designed and typeset by Blackjacks
30 Windsor Road, London W5 5PD

Colour origination by Scanners
Printed and bound in China
Produced by Mandarin Offset

For Blackjacks:
Artwork and demonstrations by Jane Wildgoose
Photography by Paul Forrester and Laura Wickenden

Credits
pp2-3 by courtesy of the Board of Trustees of the Victoria and Albert Museum;
pp10-11 © Christies Images; pp12-13 The Palace Museum, Peking;
p14 © Christies Images; p15 by courtesy of the Board of Trustees of the
Victoria and Albert Museum; pp16-17 (bottom) © John Hubbard; p17 (top left
and right) © Agnès Chevalier; p18 © Sally Greaves-Lord; p19 © Rushton Aust;
pp142-143 © Sally Greaves-Lord.

Hand-made finials and tassels for *fleur-de-lys* on pp80-81 & p97 kindly
supplied by Wendy Cushing, London

Every effort has been made to contact all copyright holders of illustrations
used in this book. If there are any omissions, we apologize in advance.

The photographs of Sally Greaves-Lord's work were kindly taken by Tim Hill.

Thanks go to Pongees of London for supplying silk, and to Sally Greaves-Lord,
Agnès Chevalier, John Hubbard and Rushton Aust for supplying photographs
and information about their work.

The author would especially like to thank Alan of George Weil and Son,
London, for his generous help and advice in the supply of silk, other materials
and equipment.

Contents

Chapter 1
Introduction

Silk is one of the most beautiful of all fibres; it is also one of the oldest. Since earliest times man (or, more often, woman) has been able to extract fine thread from the silkworm cocoon, spin it, and weave the most delicate fabric. After thousands of years and great advances in textile technology, we still prize it most highly for its delicate lustre, elegant drape and seductive feel.

The projects have been planned to give some idea of the scope of effects possible. Their subject-matter is taken from western traditions of image-making; heraldry, Italian Renaissance decorative painting, Pompeian wall paintings and seventeenth century *scagliola*. They have been chosen so that a variety of techniques can be demonstrated. They are intended as a starting point. Ultimately, when you have learnt the basic principles, the inspiration and imagery chosen can be entirely yours. There are basic rules to be learnt in order to be able to control the medium, so that you achieve the results you intend and to avoid any disappointment. Once these rules are understood, it will be up to you to experiment.

The beginner should not feel daunted. There is a project specifically designed to enable you to gain confidence in the medium. Its aim is to allow you to experience the excitement of seeing colour emerge in a new way and inspire you to find out the scope of marks you can make without the stress of trying to achieve a particular image.

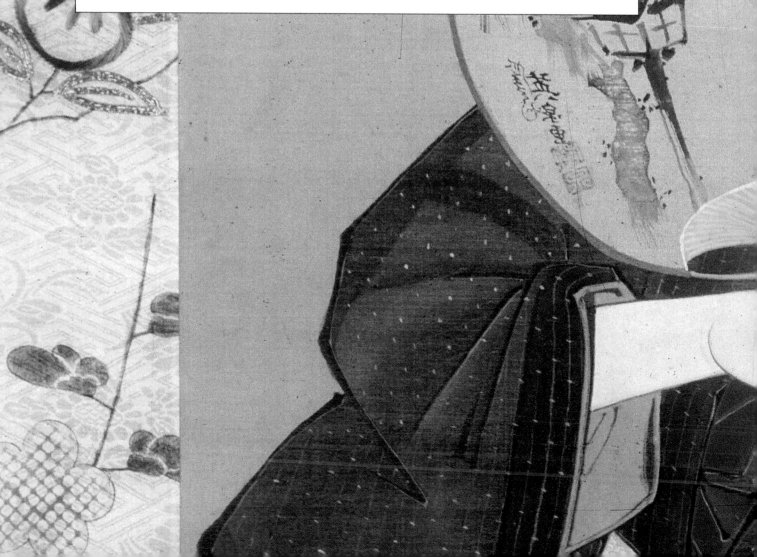

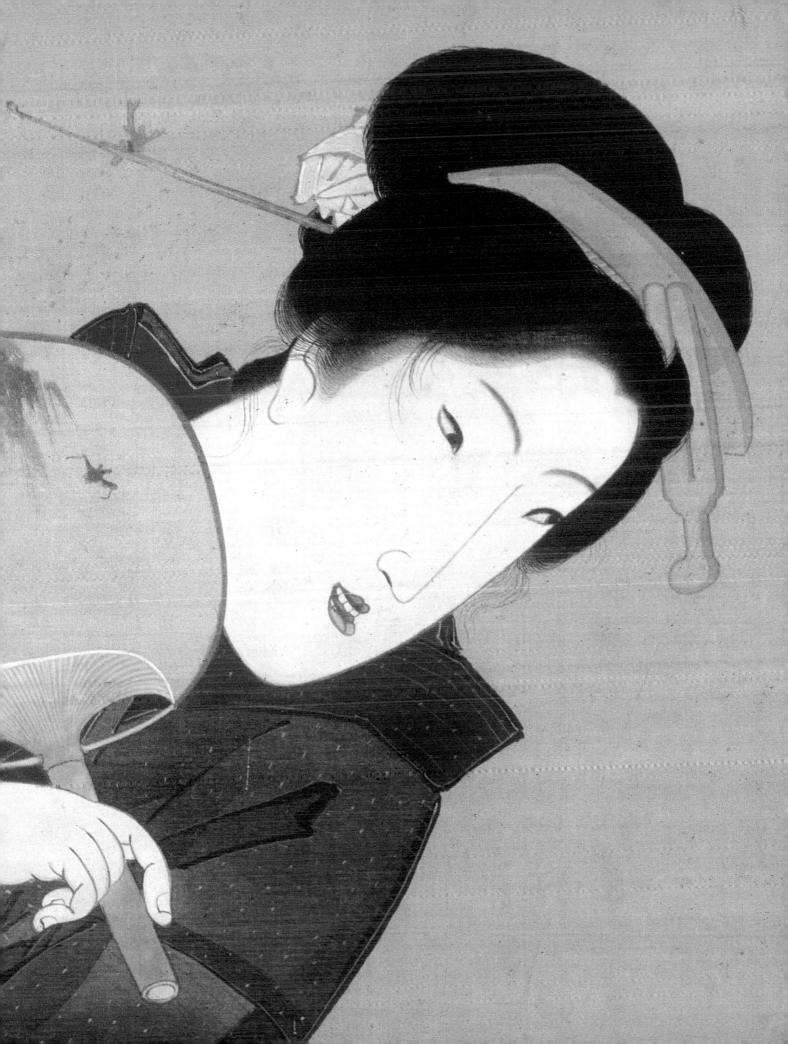

Introduction

THE ORIGINS OF PAINTING ON SILK

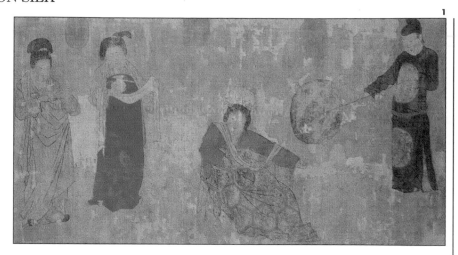

The production of silk preceded the invention of paper by at least a thousand years. Both materials were first introduced in China and it is not surprising, therefore, that the earliest examples of painting on silk are Chinese in origin. In fact, archaeological findings this century in Hunan province suggest that it can be traced back to the 4th century B.C.

The oldest form of movable painting was the hand scroll, which could be painted on either silk or paper, examples of which can be found from China and Japan. In ancient China the scroll was the oldest form of written work and the same ideograph (a Chinese character symbolizing the idea of a thing without expressing its name) was used to denote both 'painting' and 'writing'. The same brush and ink were employed for both activities. Mastery of the Chinese brush demands a high degree of control over the movements of the body and great concentration. Rhythm and vitality of brush stroke were the chief criteria of both Chinese calligraphy and painting from earliest times. It would seem logical to conclude that the form of the scroll derives from the closely linked traditions of painting and writing on

silk. Inscribed silk, mounted on wooden rods at either end, would lend itself to being rolled for storage, thus reducing it to a fraction of its length.

Hanging scrolls (probably evolved during the 7th–9th centuries) were generally displayed for quite short periods, for example, the visit of a guest, or for the duration of a season, after which the scroll would be taken down, rolled up and put away. Its form lent itself to this kind of fairly temporary display; the painting, whether on silk or paper, would be carefully mounted, with a border of silk damask or brocade, and hung from a semi-circular rod at the top, with a round pole inserted at the

bottom. This enabled the scroll to be rolled quickly and smoothly for storage in its precious container. The weight of the lower pole, whose protruding ends were usually decorated with heavy precious materials such as ivory, allowed the scroll to be weighted down sufficiently to hang flat.

The other, highly regarded form of painting on silk was that of painting on fans, the fan being a most necessary implement in countries with very humid regions. The folding fan was introduced from Japan into China in the 10th century and by the Ming dynasty (1368–1644) the format of the fan leaf became to be considered one

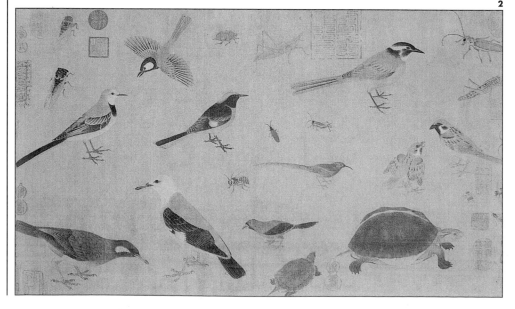

1 *Ladies Whiling Away Summer Hours*, Zhou Fang (active *c*.750–*c*.804). Handscroll 13x80½ in. (33x204.5cm).

2 *Birds, Insects and Turtles*, Huang Quan (died 965). Handscroll 16x27½ in. (40.5x70cm).

3 *Autumn Colours Over Rivers and Mountains*, Zhao Boju (active first half of 12th century). Detail of handscroll 127x22 in. (322.5x56cm).

4 *Hermitage in the Summer Mountains*, Wang Meng (*c*.1308–1385). Hanging scroll 58½x25 in. (148.5x63.5cm).

12

of the most challenging forms in which a painter could work. Some fan paintings were so highly prized that they were mounted directly on to a scroll or album leaf so that they would not be subjected to the wear and tear inflicted on them by being made up as fans.

Subject-matter for painting on silk and paper was dominated by nature, particularly the landscape. In China devout artists originally began to paint water and mountains in a spirit of reverence, to provide material for meditation. Studies of birds, fish, and insects, as well as other animals abound; often these subjects had symbolic meanings. Religious and philosophical beliefs were the inspiration of the artist, so that there

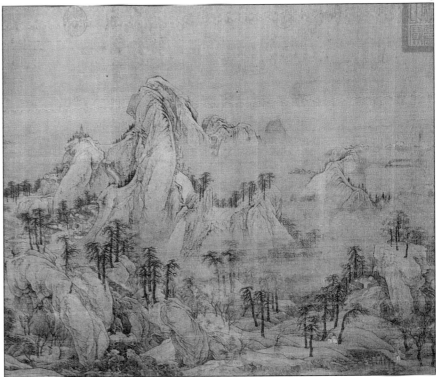

4

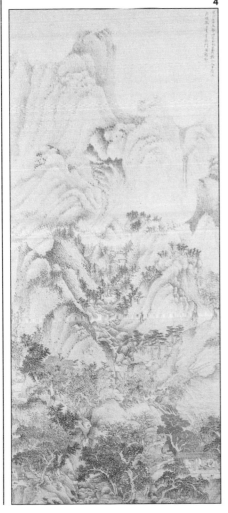

are many examples of Buddhist, Confucian, and Taoist, as well as mythological subjects. Portrait painting was largely confined to the necessities of ancestor worship and the true recording of the family line, except in the case of paintings of important historical or religious subjects, such as emperors and military leaders, philosophers, deities and mythological figures.

The Traditional Techniques

As important to the artist of the Far East as subject matter was the spirit and mood evoked by mastery of a very wide range of brush strokes. Meditation and concentration were essential to this process. Chinese artists learnt the skills of painting water, rocks, clouds and other natural phenomena by studying the works of renowned masters. Then, once they had acquired the necessary technical skill with brush and ink, they would travel and contemplate nature in order to capture its moods. The painting

would be done as soon as possible afterwards, indoors, while the vision was still fresh, to conjure up and portray the very essence of the subject and to capture the divine which exists in all things. In order to gain the required concentration and control of brush and medium, the artist undertook lengthy preparations. The time-consuming process of converting the dry, hard inksticks into liquid ink was like a religious ceremony.

Inksticks were made from deposits of soot obtained by burning vegetable oils and animal fats, which were mixed with animal glue, heated for long periods, and finely pounded before being mixed with musk and camphor to neutralize the smell. This substance was then pressed into moulds and left to harden, allowing decorations to be made on the sticks during the moulding process. Inksticks, sometimes further embellished with coloured lacquer, calligraphy or gold leaf, became highly valued in their own right, especially when matured with age,

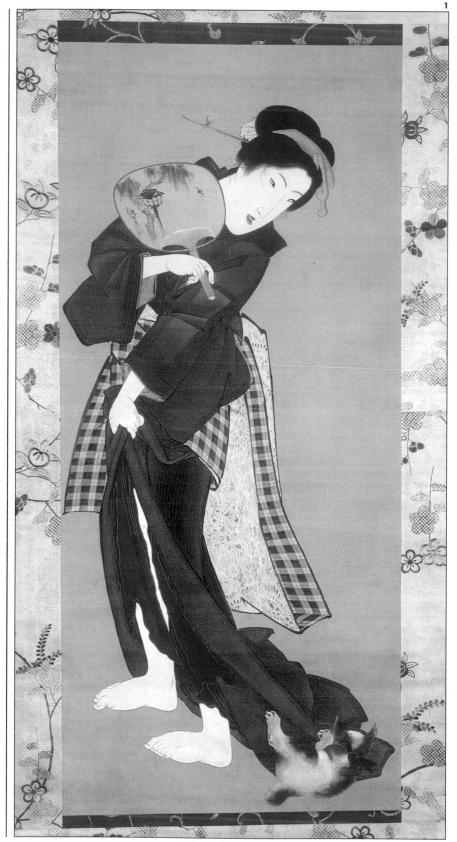

and could last many years, even when used on a regular basis.

In order to make liquid ink, the inkstick was ground with water on an inkstone (a flat slab, usually made of slate or possibly jade, with a sunken well at one end where the water was held). It was this grinding process, which was very time-consuming and repetitive in nature, that helped provide access to the spiritual grace required for the process of painting. Fresh ink would be prepared by the artist for each session. The method was used for both painting and writing on either silk or paper.

Much of the painting from the Far East employed only this black ink, but it was used in such a variety of tones and washes that it has a vivacity not usually associated with the word 'monochrome' (the term used for painting executed in different tones of the same colour). Otherwise, details were frequently added to the ink painting with colour derived from pigments of vegetable and mineral origin, ground down and mixed with glue to produce blocks not unlike inksticks in character.

Traditional methods of painting on silk persisted virtually unchanged in the Far East right up until the 19th century, when the introduction of aniline dyes (the first chemical, rather than natural, dyes, discovered in England in 1856) led to an increased range of colours available to the artist.

The Western Revival

The introduction of aniline dyes in Japan in the late 19th century coincided with the end of a 200-year period of virtual seclusion from the West. In 1854 Japan resumed trade links with Europe and America. The exported artefacts were in direct contrast to the artistic traditions which had developed in Europe. Economy and grace of line, the use of colour and evocation of mood, and the sense of balance without rigidity in the compositions, exemplified by Japanese woodblock prints in particular but also Japanese painting in general, were to have an enormous influence on painters who were questioning European academic standards. The influence of Far Eastern artistic traditions was to inform developments in the fine and decorative arts, especially in the work of the Impressionists in France and of the members of the Aesthetic Movement in England. It also helped to inspire the movement in the decorative and applied arts known as Art Nouveau.

James McNeill Whistler (1834–1903) was especially influenced by the Orientalism of much of the fine and decorative art of the end of the 19th century. A leading figure in the Aesthetic Movement, his eminence undoubtedly inspired a generation of younger artists to experiment in painting, Oriental style, on highly textured fabrics, notably silk. Outstanding among such artists were Joseph Crawhall (1861–1913) and Edwin Alexander (1870–1920), both painters of birds and animals and both associated with the Glasgow School of artists and designers.

Charles Conder (1868–1909), however, devoted himself almost entirely to painting on silk, experimenting with various materials and techniques, including watercolour, and forms – panels, fans and decorations for garments. It is perhaps Condor who is the true forerunner of the vigorous revival of interest in painting on silk in Europe and America today.

1 *Young Woman Holding a Fan*, Keisai Eisen.

2 *Scene in Seville*, Charles Conder (1868-1909).

2

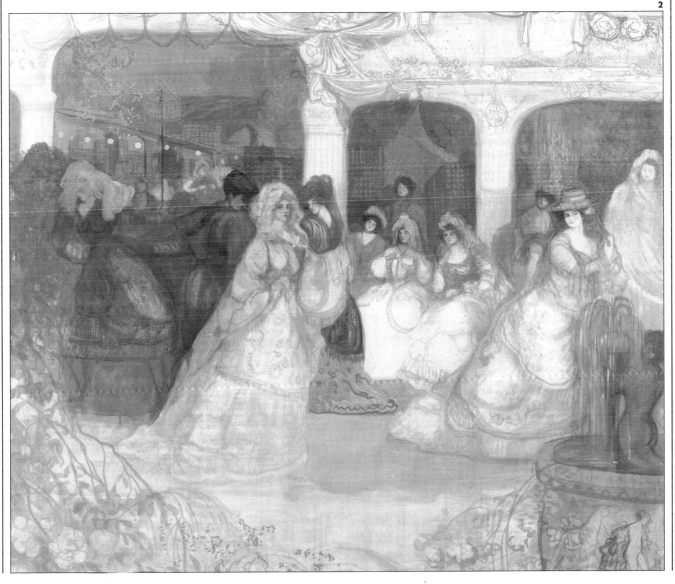

SOME CONTEMPORARY ARTISTS

The work of the contemporary artists shown in this section is unmistakably of the late 20th century, even though, in some cases, the example of the ancient Chinese painters is a strong influence.

Rushton Aust and Sally Greaves-Lord are both artists who have trained in textiles rather than painting, but combine painterly values with a strong response to the cloth on which they work. They are part of a relatively small but growing number of artists who have trained in textiles but choose to use the medium as a vehicle for one-off pieces. These include paintings on silk to be hung like traditional paintings, one-off garments, large-scale wall-hangings as part of schemes for interior decoration and more sculptural pieces. Rather than create designs for mass production in the textile industry, they combine a craftsman's understanding of his materials with an artist's ability to use those materials to convey highly personal ideas.

The painter of oils on canvas must obliterate the surface texture of the canvas by priming and stretch the canvas for painting and also for display. The textile artist chooses not to obscure the character of the fabric. Indeed, the unique quality of the silk is a vital part of any piece. By using textile media, the artist can work directly on to the surface of the silk and only mask its strong texture where appropriate. Silk may be stretched while it is being worked on, but the finished piece can be allowed to hang so that its mobility is still apparent, allowing light to play on its surface, further emphasizing the character of the fabric itself as part of the overall effect. In the work of the French artist, Agnès Chevalier, the silk is used as the medium for sculptural pieces which are also painted and dyed.

John Hubbard

John Hubbard is American but settled in England in 1961, after periods in Hokkaido and New York. While in New York he was influenced by the example of the Abstract Expressionists, but the most profound influence on his work is that of painters and poets of the classical Chinese landscape school. His continuing inspiration is the Dorset landscape. He is much influenced by the ancient Chinese tradition of the artist immersing himself in the landscape and then using a process of imaginative re-creation based on this experience to paint in the studio. He travels widely and has based a large body of work on visits to the Atlas Mountains of Morocco. His paintings have been exhibited all over the world and are held in major collections, including the Tate Gallery in London.

In the late 1980s two of his paintings were included in a group show organized by the British Council to tour Malaysia. As a result of this show he was invited by the National Gallery of Art of Kuala Lumpur to be one of an international group of artists to tour Malaysia. The artists were invited to spend the last two weeks of their stay producing pieces of work inspired by their visit.

Hubbard chose to work in batik, a traditional Malaysian form. Using dye and the *tjanting* (the little metal spouted cup attached to the end of a stick used to hold and apply melted

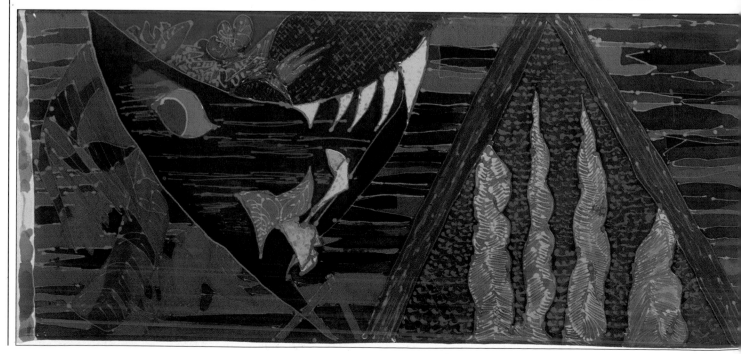

wax) presented a challenge and an inspiration. He found the character of the silk (which he used in preference to cotton) and the exotic nature of the batik factory a further inspiration. Despite primitive conditions, he produced a series of painted silk banners from notes and sketches made during the earlier part of his visit. Most of these pieces are now in collections in Malaysia, including one in the National Gallery of Art in Kuala Lumpur. The one pictured here is in the possession of the artist.

Agnès Chevalier

Agnès Chevalier trained in Fine Art at the Ecole des Beaux-Arts in Rouen, and also at the Université d'Art Plastique in Paris, with further specialization in textiles at Goldsmiths' College, London.

She designs for the theatre in France and England, as well as making sculptural and bas-relief pieces in silk, which are clearly influenced by her involvement in the theatre. She is inspired by Italian Renaissance painting and the work of the English Pre-Raphaelites and European Surrealists.

She chooses to work in silk 'because it is vibrant, alive, and especially because it is smooth and transparent like skin', building up and quilting the silk with polyester fibres, which she stitches with a very fine needle and invisible thread. She subsequently paints delicate colours with dye on the piece, or sometimes dyes the fabric before sewing when this is more appropriate.

She has exhibited her work at the Musée Jean Lurçat in Angers, the Museum of Modern Art in Strasbourg, the Anthony Dawson Fine Art Gallery in London, and regularly contributes to the Annual International Exhibitions of Miniature Art in Toronto.

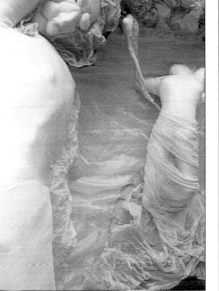

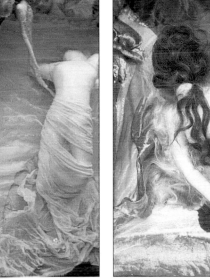

1 *A Smile Deep Within the Soul*, Agnès Chevalier.

2 *The Blowing of a Gale*, Agnès Chevalier.

3 John Hubbard, 12x3 ft. (3.66x0.91cm).

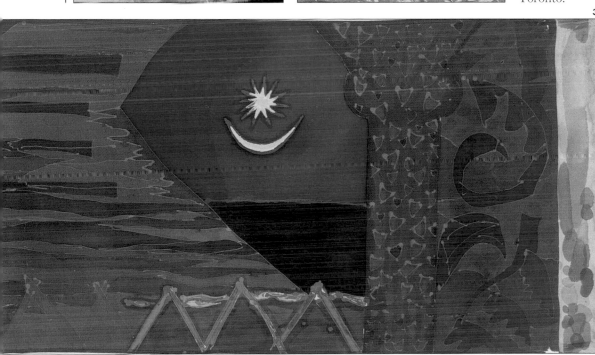

Sally Greaves-Lord

Sally Greaves-Lord trained in the department of Printed and Woven Textiles at West Surrey College of Art and Design, and went on to specialize in printed textiles at the Royal College of Art in London. She lives near the North Yorkshire moors and draws inspiration from that landscape and also from seascapes. She travels extensively to draw and paint from nature; in Italy she has been particularly inspired by the landscape of the Tuscan hills. After a drawing trip, she returns to the studio to produce hand-painted textiles, referring to the spirit of her drawings and paintings rather than making literal copies. Her latest work is inspired by the west coast of Ireland.

The rhythms of the sea are particularly apparent in these large, abstract pieces on spun silk, where the generous, expressive brush strokes contrast with formal stripes made by masking the cloth with tape prior to painting with thickened dye. The overall effect is further enhanced by her sensibility to what she calls 'the life of cloth'. Sally Greaves-Lord was Creative Director in the United Kingdom for the Japanese fashion designer Issey Miyake 1985–91, and her work was used for interiors and window displays for his British shops during that period. Her work is held in collections all over the world, including pieces in the Museums of Modern Art in Kyoto and Yokohama, as well as the Victoria and Albert Museum in London.

Rushton Aust

Rushton Aust trained in general textiles, at Derby Lonsdale College, and went on to specialize in printed textiles at the Royal College of Art. He, too, derives much inspiration from landscape, and records this in drawings, photographs and written notes and diaries, to which he refers when working on the textile pieces. He aims to capture the spirit of a place rather than make literal interpretations from his reference. He also collects found objects, both natural and man-made, as diverse as seed-heads and old bits of cars, and is moved by 'the humility of discarded objects'. Man-made detritus, he feels, often reflects

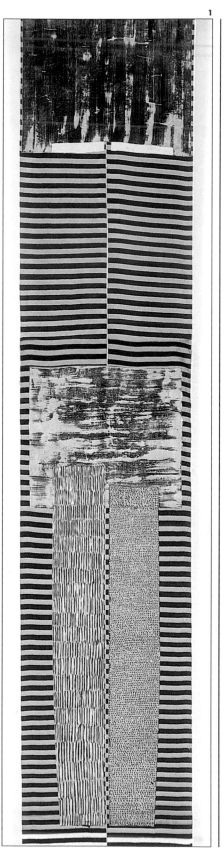

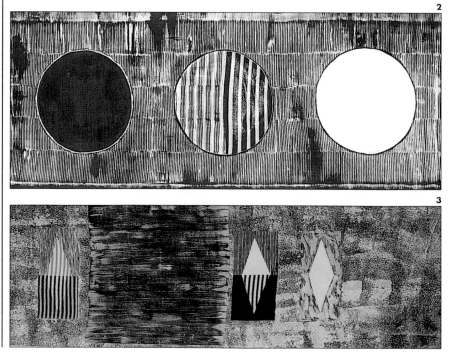

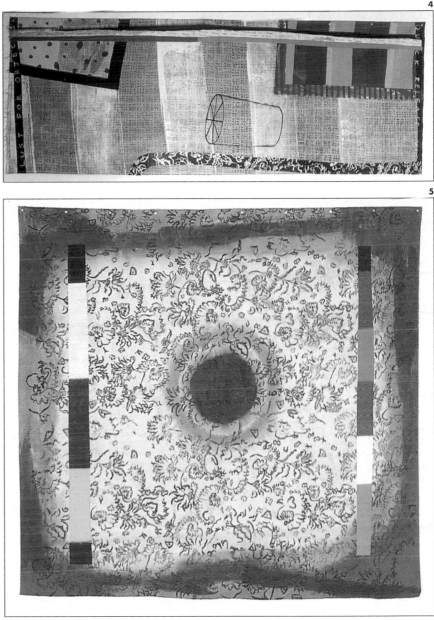

the spirit of the place where it is found. His interpretation of landscape is broad and can include such objects as tattered advertisement hoardings. By using unwanted items as subjects, he is trying to bring back to life something which has been discarded.

In his textile pieces he incorporates the inherent characteristics of the fabric, and derives a colourful vigour from using dye to paint the backgrounds. He then over-prints and paints with Helizarin colour and binder, describing the use of dye on silk as providing 'a texture and colour ripe for over-printing.'

He receives commissions from corporate clients: most recently seven pieces for the new Coca-Cola UK Headquarters in London, and a piece for British Rail Trainload Freight Division, London. His work is held in many collections, including the Museums of Modern Art in Tokyo and Kyoto, and the Stedelijk Museum in Amsterdam.

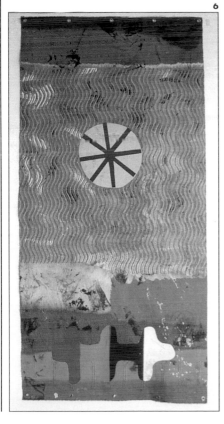

1 Sally Greaves-Lord, 36x197 in. (0.92x5m).

2 Sally Greaves-Lord, 118x36 in. (3x0.92m).

3 Sally Greaves-Lord, detail of 197x36 in. (5x0.92m).

4 Rushton Aust, 79x29½ in. (2x0.75m).

5 Rushton Aust, 59x59 in. (1.5x1.5m)

6 Rushton Aust, 19½x39 in. (0.5x1m).

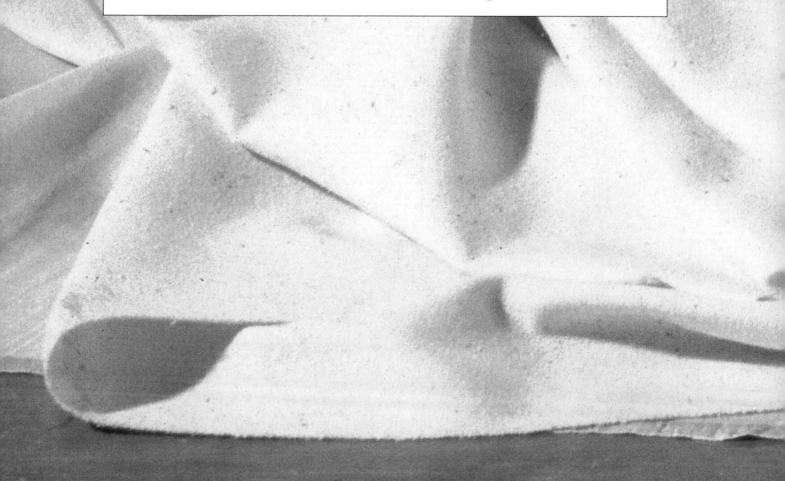

Chapter 2
Materials

All silks will readily take and retain colour if the correct medium is used. They will provide a depth and intensity of colour in combination with dye and textile pigment, which is quite different from that of paper or canvas. The lustre of the material adds a further dimension in that it reflects light and can appear to make colours really glow. White silk will take bright dye colour and make it appear more brilliant; cream or coffee coloured silk can alter the tones of colours in the most subtle ways. It is important that the correct media for use on silk are chosen. You must also learn to appreciate the properties of the media and of the silk to which you apply them. You will then achieve the best possible results.

The modern painter on silk has a wide range of chemical dyes and pigments available to him or her that are specifically designed for use on textiles. When used and fixed in the correct manner these will withstand water, dry-cleaning and the effects of light.

Textile pigments should not be confused with pigments used by painters. They are specifically designed to be used on unprimed fabric and to be washed or dry-cleaned if necessary, as long as they have been properly fixed. They differ from dyes in that they are fixed on to the surface of the fabric by dry heat.

All the dyes used in the projects in this book are intended for use on silk (and will also work on wool). They will **not** work on cotton or any other fabric. It is therefore important when using dyes to be sure that what you choose is fixed by steam and is specifically designed for the fabric you are using.

My aim is to consider ways of using modern textile media for a wide range of effects rather than concentrating on traditional methods.

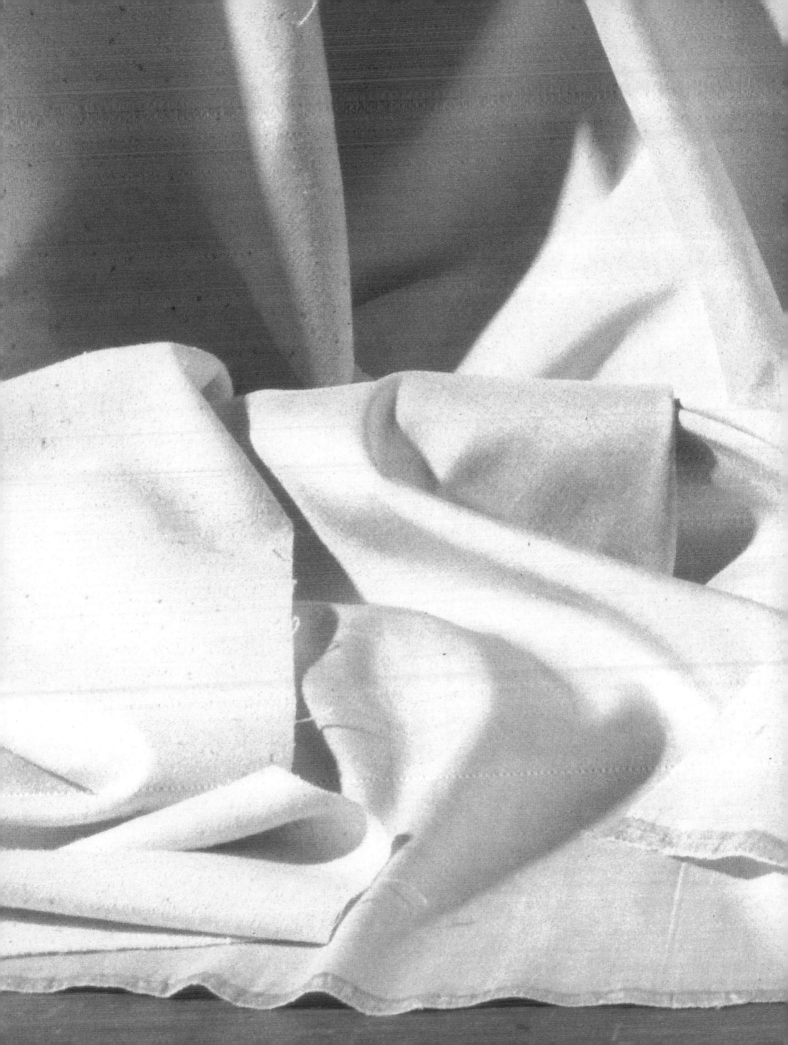

Materials

SILKS

Many legends surround the invention of sericulture. One of these suggests that a Chinese princess, while taking tea under a mulberry tree in her garden, saw a cocoon drop into her cup. The hot liquid softened and loosened the cocoon. When the princess, in her curiosity, pulled on the end of the fibre which emerged, she discovered it to be one long, continuous silken thread.

This legend provides us with the basic information about silk production. The *Bombyx mori*, a silkworm which thrives upon mulberry leaves, has developed silk glands along the underside of its body by the time it reaches maturity. Its rich diet of mulberry leaves causes these glands to become engorged with fluid which is ejected through a spinneret in the lower lip of the worm's mouth. This causes a cocoon to be formed of a single, continuous thread for protection during the pupa stage. This thread hardens and dries as it is exposed to the air. The spinning of the cocoon takes between three and five days and, depending on the genetic background of the silkworm, will be white, creamish, or yellow.

After about two weeks the pupa will have developed wings and sufficient strength to emerge from the cocoon, thus breaking its continuous thread. It is therefore necessary to kill the pupa before this stage is reached. Traditionally pupae were killed by exposure to very hot sun, immersion in boiling water, or by placing in hot ovens. Nowadays it is more likely the pupae will have been killed by high frequency radio waves; these have the advantage of killing the pupae instantly and not affecting the silk.

On average the silk thread harvested from a single cocoon of the *Bombyx mori* is between 800-1200 yards (730-1100m). The cocoons are immersed in boiling water, which dissolves the substance which holds together the silk threads. The cocoon softens and the long, continuous silk thread loosens and floats in the water,

SILKS

where it can be collected and reeled. It is then spun, and subsequently woven, to produce a fabric of unparalleled beauty and rich diversity.

There are many different types of silk, all with different characteristics, and it is well worth considering which silk would best suit the ideas you wish to paint before you commence.

Silk ranges from the finest, most diaphanous fabrics – georgette, chiffon and habotai – to quite coarse, slubby silks.

Illustrated on the previous spread is a group of silks which are spun and woven to produce flat, even surfaces with varying degrees of lustre. The range of colours and tones is especially fine and subtle, from bright, bleached white through cream to coffee. The group of flat silks include habotai, taffeta, and spun taffeta.

The group of silks illustrated on this spread have the slubs (irregular little bumps which occur in the thread taken from the silk cocoon) incorporated in the woven fabric. These silks are generally unbleached and tend to be darker than flat silks. The range of natural tones is an inspiring palette in itself. Included in this group are: noile, with its characteristic fine, dark fleck; tussah, with small, irregular slubs; douppion, with larger, irregular slubs and an otherwise shiny surface; and herring-bone, with distinctive golden streaks in the herring-bone pattern of the weave. Even the matte surfaces have a subtle gleam.

Ideally, silk should be washed to remove any impurities which will resist the colour applied. Before you commence painting, wash the silk in warm, soapy water and rinse thoroughly before drying naturally.

Iron the silk, on the wrong side, while it is still damp. If it does dry completely then it can be ironed by the following method to avoid marking. Lay a clean sheet of brown paper over the entire surface of the silk; place a damp piece of muslin of the same size over the paper; then iron as usual without steam.

COLOURS FOR USE ON TEXTILES

Colours for use on textiles fall into two groups: dyes and pigments. There are two types of pigment: colour mixed with binder, and 'ready-to-use', which requires no mixing and is fixed by dry heat. They each have different properties and can be used on their own or in conjunction with one another to produce very varied effects on silk. When using different processes on the same piece it is important to understand at which stage each process will need to be fixed and how it should be fixed.

Dyes

Dyes are available in both powder and liquid form. In powder form, dyes require certain chemicals to be added in order to be effective. Therefore liquid dyes, ready prepared for use on silk, are used throughout this book.

They are recommended to the small-scale painter on silk as they are convenient to use and present the least hazard to health (see 'Health and Safety' opposite).

When used properly, dyes produce translucent, glowing colours which are further enhanced by the lustre of the silk. Used undiluted it is possible to obtain a brilliance of colour quite unlike that produced by any

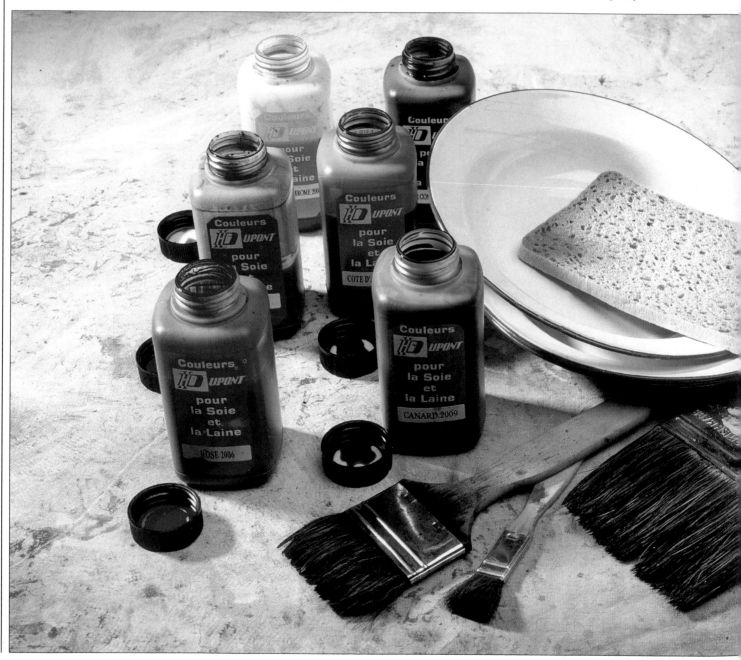

other media. Dyes can be diluted with water to produce any tone, down to the palest washes. These dyes are intermixable. Used alone, or with water, dyes will spread or 'bleed'. If this is not required, then the dye can be thickened with ready prepared thickener, or with Manutex F (see page 43). The disadvantage of using dyes is that they remain susceptible to water until they have been steamed.

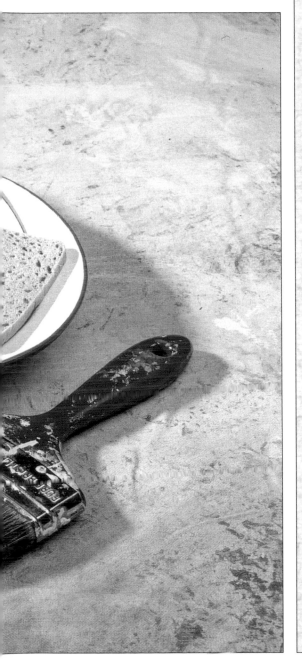

Health and Safety

Spirit- and solvent-free media have been chosen as far as possible for use in this book because they represent the least hazard to health. Where there is a choice, it is better to opt for media which are spirit- and solvent-free. Even so, all textile media are chemically based and should, therefore, be treated in a responsible manner. It is essential that you observe the following points when handling and storing textile media:

● Store all textile media out of the reach of children, in a locked cupboard, or on a high shelf out of reach.

● Always wear rubber gloves if your hands are going to come into contact with the media. Wear an apron or suitable overall to protect your clothes, depending on the scale of your work.

● Store and use textile media well away from food. Do not eat, drink, or smoke when using the media.

● Even if you have been wearing rubber gloves, wash your hands before coming into contact with food or drink, or smoking, and before using the lavatory.

● Always follow the manufacturers' instructions for the safe use of any media or equipment you may use.

● It is *absolutely essential* that any items of equipment generally associated with food or other domestic use are kept *only* for use with textiles or other crafts. *Never* subsequently use them for food.

● Always clean up thoroughly after work, using cloths or sponges reserved for use with textile media. If possible, have a separate workplace for textile media, well away from any area used for food preparation. The place where you work with textile media should be well ventilated.

● Keep all your media in their original containers and make sure they are clearly labelled. If you must transfer the media into a different container, ensure that any previous labelling has been completely removed or obliterated and that the container is clearly labelled with its new contents.

COLOURS FOR USE ON TEXTILES

Pigments

Textile pigments are quite different from artists' pigments, and are specially designed for use on textiles. They are available in two types: those mixed with a special binder, and those ready prepared which can be painted on silk without the addition of binder. They are fixed by dry heat, which makes them simple to use. They do have varying degrees of opacity, however, and the two types behave quite differently.

Helizarin Colours and Bricoprint Binder SF20

This medium was originally developed for silk-screen printing on textiles, hence its viscous nature. For years it was only available in bulk, but has become available in smaller quantities suitable for use by the textile painter. The bottles of Helizarin colour illustrated here would last most silk painters a lifetime; the colours are extremely concentrated and only a very small amount is required to make even the strongest colours. If you have problems with availability then silk-screen media for use on textiles in schools would generally have similar properties, as do some of the more opaque, ready-to-use pigments available to the silk painter.

Helizarin colours are designed to be used in conjunction with a special binder: a white emulsion which carries the colour. This particular binder has been chosen as it is solvent free. The colour is mixed into the binder and used either full strength or in dilution, depending on the proportion of colour to binder used. Helizarin colour and binder are fixed by dry heat: solvent-free binder and colour can be fixed by ironing after the colour has dried for 5 minutes, on the cotton setting, on the wrong side of the silk. Alternatively, small pieces can be fixed for 5 minutes at 400°F in a small electric oven kept specially for textile use (see 'Health and Safety' page 27). Very fine silk should be protected by being loosely wrapped in calico. The pigment is bonded by dry heat to the surface of the fabric. It is fairly opaque and therefore tends to mask the surface quality of the silk. The colours are illustrated here with Bricoprint SF20 in the enamel dish. For more opaque, pastel colours, the Helizarin colours can be mixed into Bricoprint Opaque White T, or other opaque white for use on silk. Because the binder is so viscous it tends to sit on the surface of the silk without spreading. To produce a more stain-like effect, the mixture can be diluted with up to an equal quantity of water.

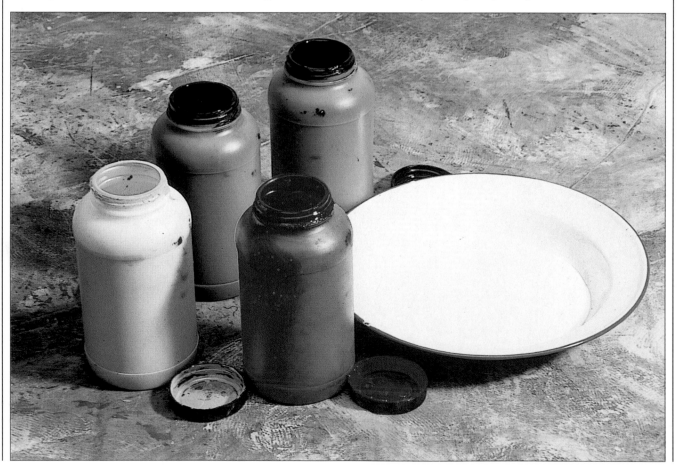

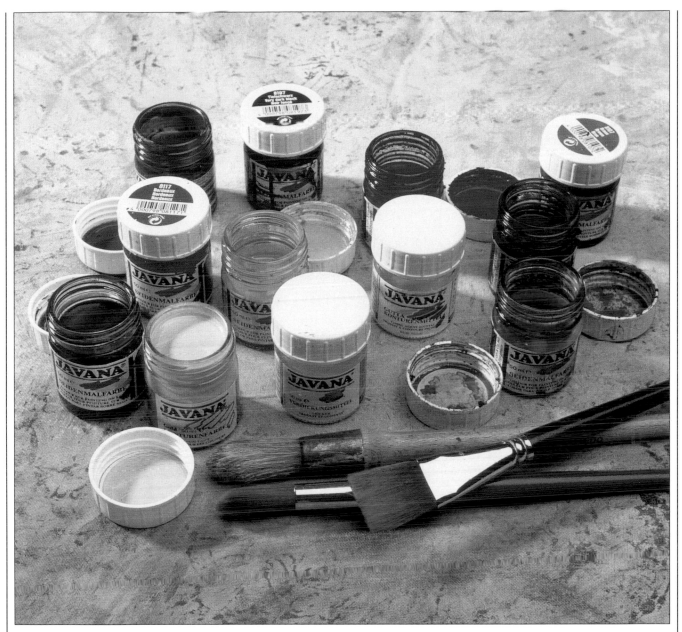

Ready-to-Use Pigments

Ready-to-use textile pigments, such as the ones illustrated here, combine the advantages of being fixed very simply – either by ironing or, in the case of a newly developed range, by hanging – with a less opaque effect than Helizarin colours and binder. Designed specially for the silk painter, they are also readily available in small quantities. They do not have the extreme brilliance of dyes, but they are simple and direct to use. They are intermixable and can be used diluted with water for pale shades, or at full strength. Used on their own or diluted with water, they will spread like watercolour and can be mixed wet on wet. They can also be mixed with ready-to-use thickener, so that painted forms retain their shape without spreading or 'bleeding'. They can also be used with a textile primer (see page 53).

The range of colours illustrated here, while not being as translucent as dye, comes a very close second. They have the advantage of not having to be steamed. Other ready-to-use pigments are more opaque and could be used instead of the Helizarin colour and binder. This is especially important where chalky pastel colours are required and colour can be mixed into opaque white. You will probably have to experiment with several different brands before you are confident about what the final effect will be.

SUPPORTS

In order to be able to paint on silk without it moving, the fabric has to be stretched for the application of colour. It may be necessary to remove the silk from time to time for fixing procedures, but it must always be re-stretched before any more colour is applied.

There are two main methods of stretching silk for painting: over a wooden frame; or over a flat, slightly padded surface, such as a board or table, depending on the size of the piece of silk on which you intend to work.

Frames

Frames are useful for stretching silk when painting backgrounds. They allow air to circulate freely so that the silk dries relatively quickly. They can also be adjusted to suit the size of silk on which you are working. They do, however, tend to move, making detailed painting difficult (unless you have an easel), especially since the silk is already inclined to move as you paint on it. It is generally a good idea to transfer work on to a padded board or table for detailed painting. Wooden frames are available ready-made, but they are simple enough to make for anyone with a basic knowledge of woodwork.

There are two main types of adjustable frame. There is the traditional wooden frame originally used for batik; this is of very simple construction and consists of four strips of wood with notches cut out of them. This frame requires no fixings. The second type is fitted together with screws which fit into slots in the wooden slats. The silk is then attached to the frame with drawing pins or special three pronged pins.

Make the frame 2 in. (5cm) bigger than the piece you intend to paint and cut the silk correspondingly oversized so that the edges of your work do not get damaged. It is a good idea to completely cover the wooden frame with plastic parcel tape so that it does not become stained with colour which might be transferred on to pieces of silk subsequently stretched on the frame.

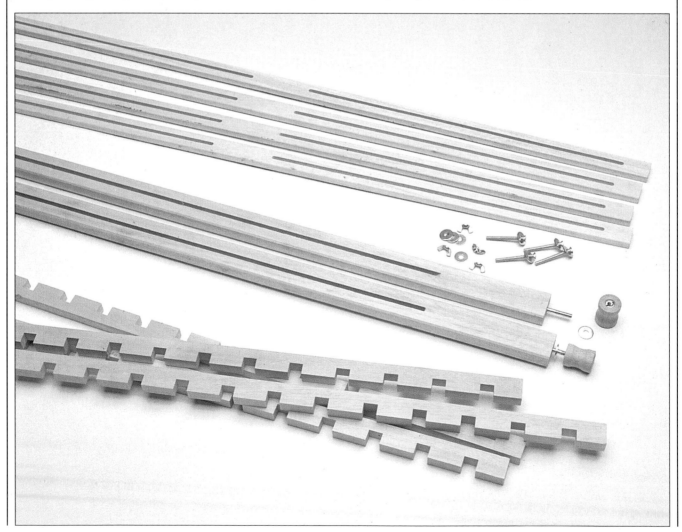

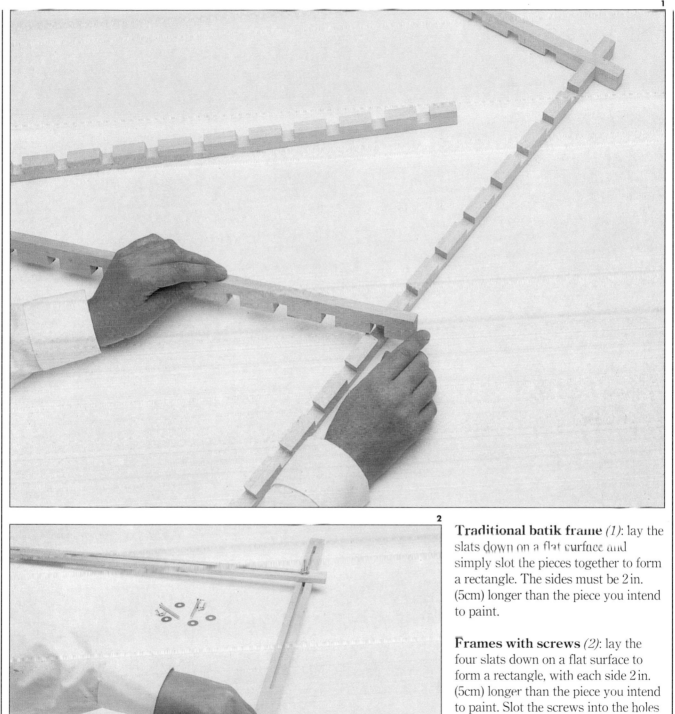

Traditional batik frame *(1)*: lay the slats down on a flat surface and simply slot the pieces together to form a rectangle. The sides must be 2 in. (5cm) longer than the piece you intend to paint.

Frames with screws *(2)*: lay the four slats down on a flat surface to form a rectangle, with each side 2 in. (5cm) longer than the piece you intend to paint. Slot the screws into the holes in the slats and tighten.

SUPPORTS

Padding A Board

To provide a good surface on which to paint silk, it is well worth taking the trouble to pad a board or table. If you are only painting detail in pigment (i.e. textile media fixed by dry heat) it may be sufficient only to stretch underfelt or an old blanket on a board as not much colour will go through onto the board. If necessary, this can be fixed by ironing after the silk has been removed and before the board is used again. Any dye or pigment left on the board or its covering – particularly dye – will be liable to transfer on to the next piece of silk as soon as it is made wet with painting. A slightly padded surface makes painting easier. Plastic is put over the padding to protect it, this in turn is covered with calico. Backgrounds on thicker silks can be painted stretched over a board padded in this way. Just allow more time for drying.

1   Use a board at least 2 in. (5cm) larger all round than the piece of silk on which you intend to paint. Lay the board down on a piece of underfelt, old blanket, or polyester wadding, and mark around the edges. Cut out leaving a further margin, sufficient to cover one side of the board and stretch over the edge to be attached on the back.

2   Place the board on the underfelt where you have marked it. Starting on one long side attach the underfelt to the board using a staple gun and staples spaced approximately 1½in. (4cm) apart.
   Then work on the opposite side, making sure you have pulled the underfelt tight and that there are no creases on the other side (which will be the surface on which you work).

3   Repeat stapling on the two short sides. Trim the corners with a pair of sharp scissors.

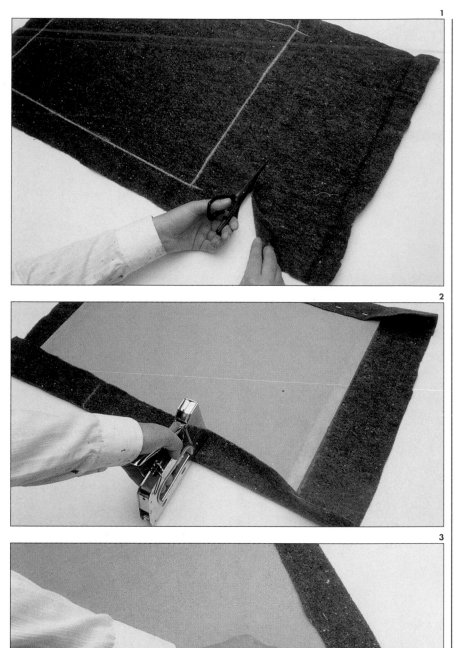

4 Lay the padded board on a piece of plastic large enough to repeat steps 1, 2 and 3, this time marking, cutting and attaching the plastic to the board.

5 Repeat with a clean piece of calico. Turn over the board and it is now ready for use. If, when you remove the silk from the board after painting a piece, the calico has dye on it, wash the calico in very hot, soapy water; rinse, dry and iron, then it can be re-used. If there is colour on the plastic, wipe it with a damp sponge or cloth and dry before replacing the clean calico.

6 To stretch the silk on the board, lay the freshly ironed silk flat on the clean, padded board. Ensure that one long side of the silk is parallel with one of the long sides of the board and secure with masking tape, leaving as few gaps in the tape as possible. Make sure that the silk is quite flat. Press the tape down firmly. Pull the silk on the opposite side from that which you have secured with tape, starting in the middle and working outwards, securing with masking tape as you go. Repeat on the two short sides, pulling the last edge slightly to remove any wrinkles in the silk. You are now ready to paint.

BRUSHES

Any brush can be used for painting on silk, depending on the type of mark you intend to make. The brushes shown here give some indication of the range from which you might choose. As you become more familiar with the media, you will probably develop preferences for particular kinds of brushes or other utensils for applying colour (see page 44).

It is generally advisable not to buy the most expensive artists' brushes, as the use of the textile media (particularly Helizarin colour and binder) will require rigorous washing which tends to shorten the life of the brush. Dyes, because they are so concentrated, are also very difficult to wash out of brushes. Beware of traces of colour left on the brush after washing, these may reactivate – even after they have been left to dry – and mix into any colour subsequently used on the brush. Yellow dye is particularly susceptible to being tainted in this way. Listed below is a recommended range of basic brushes.

Soft round brushes
These are flexible and appropriate for sinuous fine lines where a good deal of control is required, particularly for small detail. The basic range includes 0 or 00; no. 2 or no. 3; no. 6 or no. 8; no. 12.

Soft flat brushes
These are available in very soft hair, with flat wooden handles, or with firmer hair which is not as tough as bristle. The latter are easier to control and can be ideal for flowing lines, while the former, in larger sizes, are useful for backgrounds: ½ in. (1.5cm); 1in. (2.5cm); 2½ in. (6cm).

Flat bristle brushes
These tend to separate when used with textile media, giving distinctive streaked marks.

A 4 in. (10cm) decorators' bristle brush
This is extremely useful for backgrounds, particularly if you want to blend colours in large areas or if you want to make big, broad brush marks.

A medium sized stippling brush
This is also useful if you want to use stencils, or it can be used freehand (see also page 55).

Other Equipment
Illustrated here is a group of miscellaneous items useful to the painter on silk.

One of the most important items is a pair of rubber gloves (see 'Health and Safety' page 27). You will also need an apron or other form of overall (depending on the scale of your work), kept specifically for craft use.

Clingfilm is useful for covering palettes if colours have to be left for more than a short time, as it helps to prevent the media from deteriorating.

A large roll of kitchen towel is invaluable, both for mopping up colour which is behaving unpredictably on the painting, and for colour which behaves all too predictably if spilt. All colours for use on textiles are highly concentrated and will stain many surfaces other than fabric. It is wise to cover surfaces where you work with plastic before you commence.

Because textile colours stain other materials so easily, a porcelain palette, although considerably more expensive than plastic, is a worthwhile investment, as plastic palettes do get very stained.

Inexpensive enamel dishes are very useful when painting large areas such as backgrounds. They do not stain and easily accommodate large brushes. They can also be useful as palettes when you wish to mix colours as you work.

Masking tape can be used very easily to make neat borders or for masking geometric shapes for subsequent painting.

For measuring or mixing large amounts of colour, particularly Helizarin colour and binder, you may need to use a spoon. Stainless steel is preferable. Any spoons or other domestic utensils usually used with food should be kept for craft use **only**.

If a pressure cooker is used for steaming dyed colour, or a small oven for baking Helizarin colour and binder, it must be kept **only** for craft use and **never** subsequently used for food.

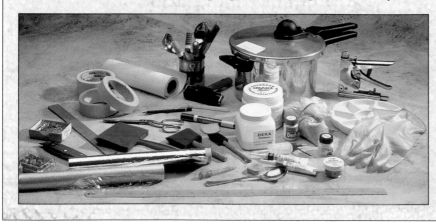

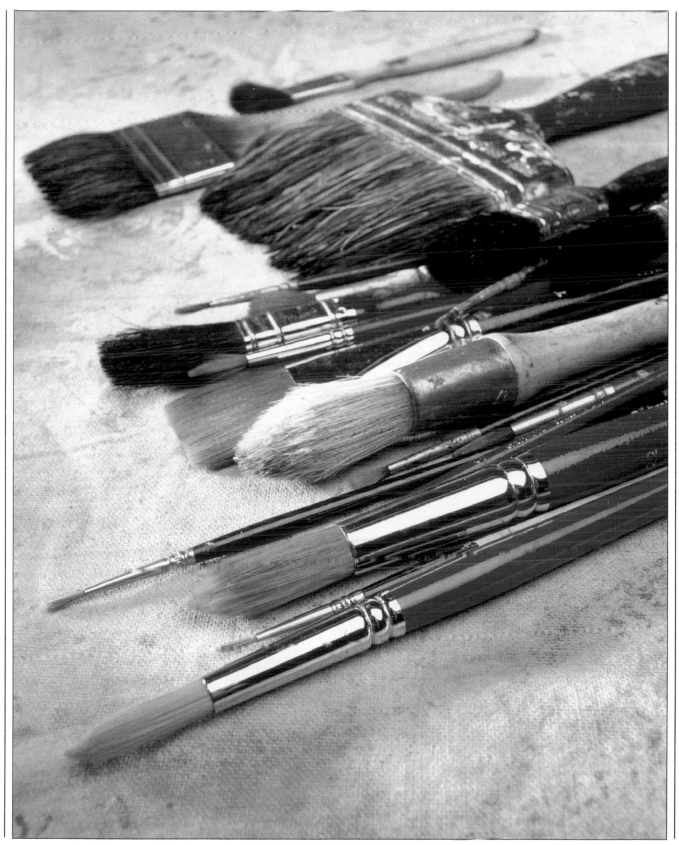

Chapter 3
Techniques

The range of techniques available to the silk painter is extremely wide, and made even more varied by the surface of the silk. As well as being able to use three different types of media with different properties (dyes, ready-to-use pigment and Helizarin colour mixed with binder) the effects you can achieve are quite different if you apply the same methods and media to different types of silk. For instance, habotai is very fine, smooth, and shiny. It is easily flooded with dye; colours applied to it with dye appear particularly bright and intense because of its lustre. Its smooth surface allows fine, unbroken lines to be applied with brush or felt-tip pen for textile use. Douppion, by contrast, has large, irregular slubs which break up painted or drawn lines. It is thicker than habotai and so absorbs more colour, which means that even when painting with unthickened dye the colour does not spread so much.

In the section of this chapter on brush strokes the examples have each been painted on both habotai and douppion to show how the surface of the cloth affects the marks put on it. The other techniques are demonstrated on unbleached taffeta. Almost any mark can be reproduced on silk. It will only take you a little while to get used to the way that the silk behaves and to find out the limitations, as well as the possibilities, of the media.

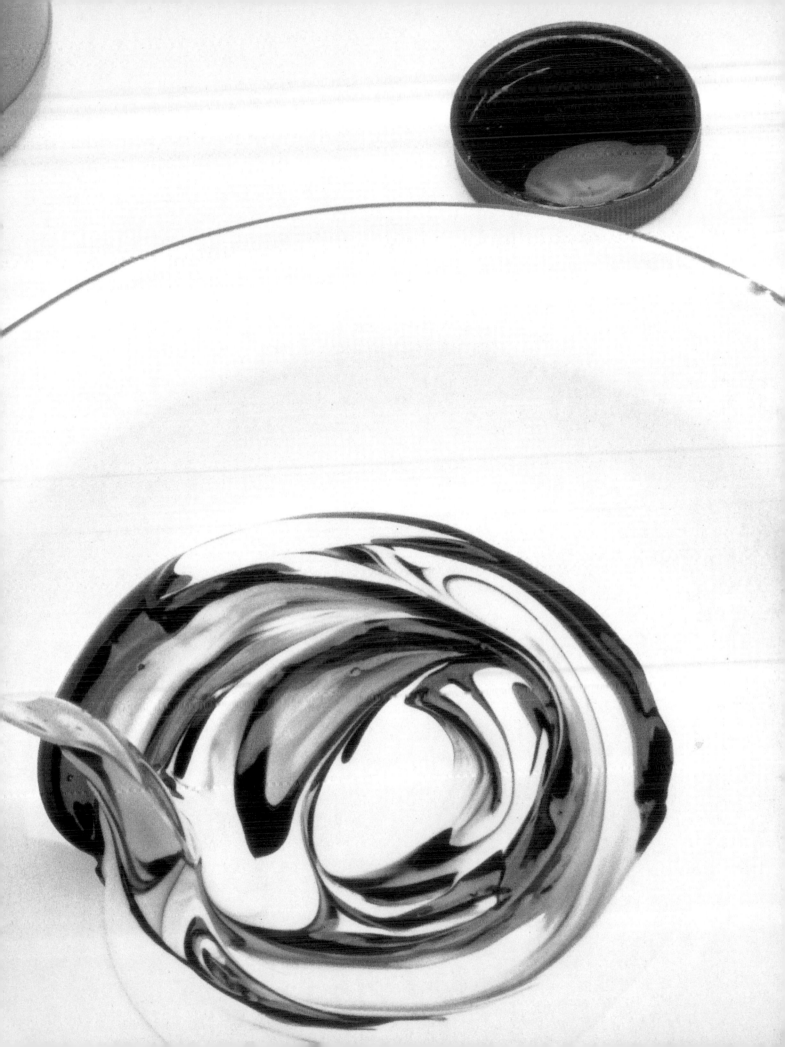

Techniques

USING COLOUR

Dyes and pigments are available in an amazingly wide range of colours. It can be tempting to buy a large selection of colours, but then be shocked by the cost.

With a little knowledge of colour theory, it is possible to mix virtually every colour you will need using a very small selection of colours. These should include: The three primary colours: blue, red, and yellow and should be as 'pure' as possible. In other words, each of these colours should not appear to have any of the others mixed into it. The yellow should not appear too orange or too green; the blue should not appear too violet or too green; the red should not appear too orange or too violet.

In addition to these three primaries you will need magenta, turquoise, brown and black. White is available in pigment and can give very different effects to your painting, depending on whether it is of the opaque type, or a more translucent type for mixing.

There is, of course, no white dye. Lighter shades of colours are obtained by diluting with water (which can provide the most subtle shades).

It is a good idea when first purchasing colours, whether dye or pigment, to stretch some small swatches on to a padded board and to experiment with the colours as follows: full strength; in dilution; mixed together, and so on. Make a note of the quantities used next to the colours with indelible biro. Fix in the appropriate manner; wash and iron. The colours may change a little during the fixing and washing processes, so it is important to follow these procedures so that you are confident of the final colour you will achieve.

It can be very helpful to keep a notebook of swatches of colour like this, labelled with the make of dye or pigment and the name of the colour used, along with any other special information, (for instance, whether the silk has been washed prior to painting or not). Even if some of the colours you mix do not come out as you anticipate, it quite often happens that these 'mistakes' provide inspiration for the future. You can keep adding to the notebook as you do the projects, with every colour first tested on a scrap of fabric, labelled, and added to the record.

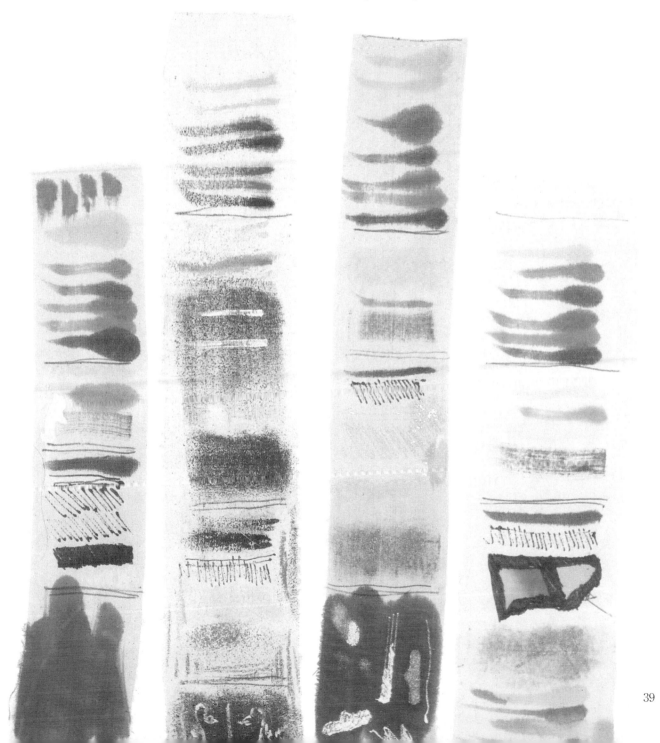

COLOUR MIXING

In-depth colour theory is outside the scope of this book, but the following guidelines are useful.

Primary Colours		*Secondary Colours*
yellow+red	=	orange
yellow+blue	=	green
red+blue	=	violet

Very roughly speaking, if you mix any two of the three primary colours together, then the primary colour left out will be the complementary colour of the secondary colour you have mixed: yellow + red = orange, which is the complementary of blue; yellow + blue = green, which is the complementary of red; red + blue = violet, which is the complementary of yellow.

True complementary colours are those which fall opposite one another on the colour wheel and which, when mixed together, yield a blackish grey, but it is helpful to know this rough grouping.

When true complementary colours are painted next to each other the effect is dazzling, as the two colours appear to vibrate. When complementary colours are mixed together they cancel one another out, producing a neutral colour.

Thus, it is possible to make bright colours duller to produce more neutral effects, depending on the proportions of colour used. In this way you don't always have to resort to black to produce grey, although it can be useful for shading or darkening colours.

Ochre can be mixed by taking bright yellow and adding a tiny amount of violet (its complementary). Bright red can be mixed to make brown by the addition of green, or, by adding less green, the red can be modified and neutralized, producing a duller shade of red, and so on.

You can experiment by mixing as many colours and shades as possible, using only the primary colours to produce the following shades: lime-green; bottle-green; orange; brick; blue-violet; red-violet; ochre; grey; brown.

Try these out on small swatches of different types of silk and you will be able to see to what extent the colour of the silk affects the colour painted on to it.

Mixing Grey from Primary Colours Using Ready-to-Mix Pigments

Javana silk paints are used here: Cherry (8194); Lapis Blue (8195); Intense Sun Yellow (8122). These three colours were chosen as being the closest available to pure colours. The colour used here was mixed for painting the background in the Black 'Pompeian' project (see page 106). For this exercise you will only require very small amounts of colour in a palette with small individual containers.

Start with the blue and add a small amount of red. Stir thoroughly *(1)*. This will make a purple colour, the secondary colour from the two primaries.

Then add a little yellow *(2)*, the complementary of the purple you have just mixed. The purple will darken and neutralize. Stir well. If the colour looks too green, add a little more red *(3)* to neutralize. Stir well.

The final colour *(4)* will be greenish-grey. It will not have the intensity of a manufactured black, but it is possible to mix greys by this method to have their own colour 'feel': red-based, blue-based, or green-based. These can be used to complement the colours you are using or in conjunction with a manufactured black. (See the Black 'Pompeian' project, page 106, where this grey is used to give depth to a manufactured black.)

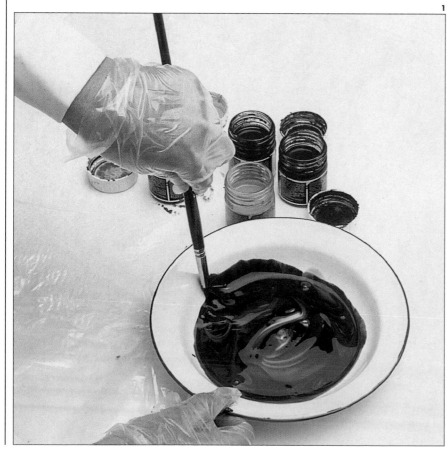

1

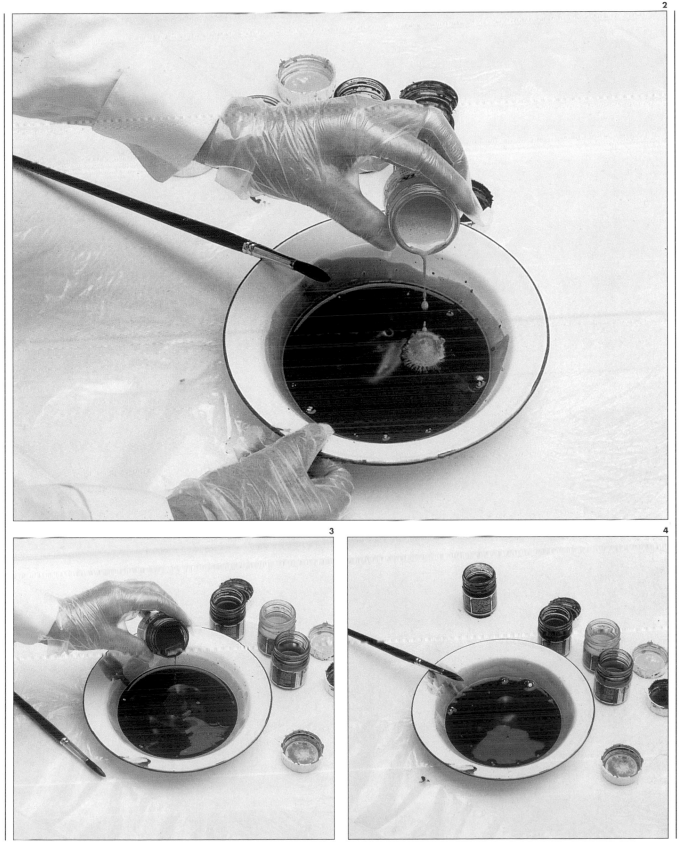

COLOUR MIXING

Mixing Black Using Helizarin Colour and Bricoprint Binder SF20

Helizarin colours are not used on their own. They require mixing with a binder (Bricoprint Binder SF20 is used here) or opaque white. This method is the one followed for mixing any Helizarin colour or mixture of colours and binder. (The black mixed here is sufficient for a background. For this exercise mix very small amounts in a palette with small containers.)

Pour a little of the Bricoprint Binder SF20 into the palette. Add a very small amount of Helizarin Black TT *(1)* or other colour(s) chosen. These colours are extremely concentrated and very small amounts should be added at a time to avoid over-saturating the mixture.

Mix thoroughly *(2)* until no traces of the white binder remain. Very intense black *(3)* can be achieved with Helizarin colour and binder. Grey can be mixed, using less Helizarin Black in the mixture with the binder, or by using a mixture of 'primary' colours in the binder instead of black.

A much more chalky, pastel grey can be achieved by mixing the Helizarin Black TT into Bricoprint Opaque White T instead of the binder.

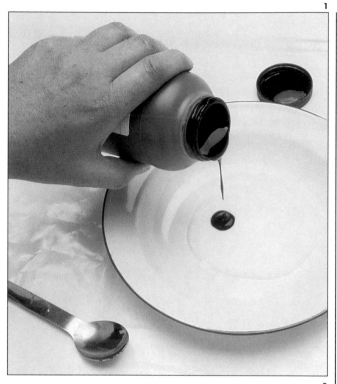

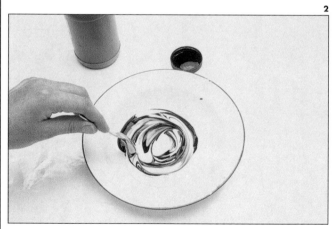

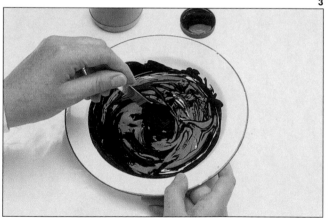

Mixing Dyes

Dyes can be mixed, or diluted with water, in a palette with small containers for small areas, or in an enamel dish for larger areas. An eye dropper is strongly recommended for transferring small amounts of dye into the palette, as it is not very easy to pour directly from the bottles. You might like to try mixing the 'primaries' to make grey and comparing it with the effect you achieved with pigment.

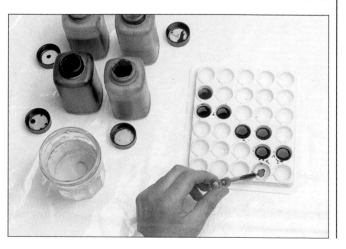

Mixing Dye With Manutex

Dye is not sticky like Helizarin colour and binder. It needs to be thickened if you do not want it to spread, and if you want to be able to control the marks you make. You can use ready prepared thickener which is mixed into the dye in a proportion of one part thickener to four parts dye, or you can use Manutex. When mixing ready prepared thickener into dye it is necessary to mix very thoroughly: nothing appears to happen for some time while you are mixing and then, suddenly, the dye thickens.

Manutex is an alginate gum and comes in powder form. It is simple to mix and can be kept mixed in an airtight container. Storage times vary according to conditions, from a few days to a few weeks. It is best to mix up small quantities at a time at first and find out how long it will keep. It is inclined to go mouldy if kept for too long.

Manutex F is used here with the Dupont dyes used in the projects. Into 250mls water sprinkle 1-2 teaspoons Manutex F *(1)*, as if you were mixing wallpaper paste. Stir very thoroughly *(2)* until all the lumps have disappeared. This mixture can be thinned with water or thickened with more Manutex, depending on your requirements. Mix the Manutex mixture thoroughly with the dye *(3)* until it is the required consistency for painting.

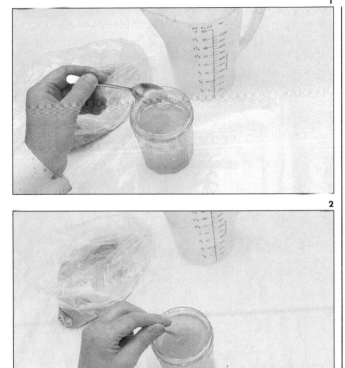

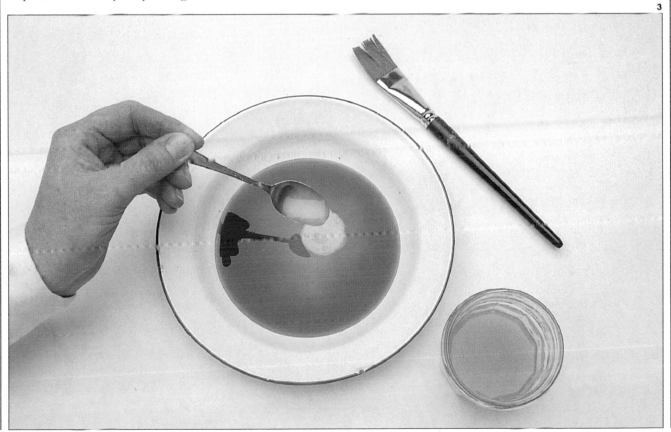

BRUSH STROKES

All the examples of brush strokes shown here are demonstrated on habotai and douppion to give some indication of the way the quality of the silk affects the results of any given technique. It is possible to use virtually any brush or other utensil usually used for applying paint to paper or canvas, but you will need to spend some time getting used to the way the silk responds and how the media behave when used on different types of silk. The examples use different media to show the variations in the way they behave.

1 Unthickened dye is used with an 0 brush; because the dye is very fluid it spreads as it is applied to the silk, spreading more rapidly on the fine habotai than on the thicker douppion.

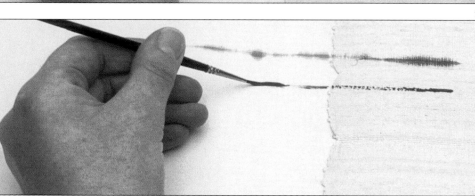

2 The same brush is used with Helizarin colour mixed with binder. The mixture is quite viscous and therefore the colour does not spread. It is possible to make much more controlled marks than with the unthickened dye.

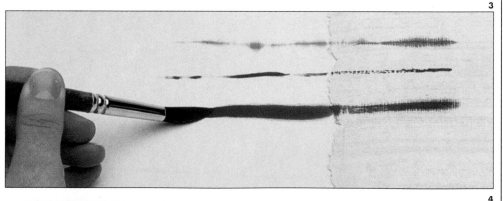

3 A soft no. 12 brush is used with unthickened dye. Because the brush holds quite a lot of dye, it is quickly absorbed as soon as the brush comes into contact with the silk, where it spreads rapidly, especially on the fine habotai. This can be used for watercolour effects where washes of colour are required.

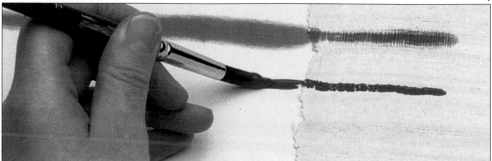

4 Helizarin colour and binder with the no. 12 brush, by contrast, can be used to make large, controlled marks.

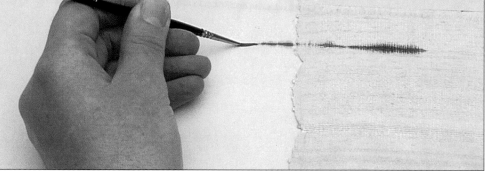

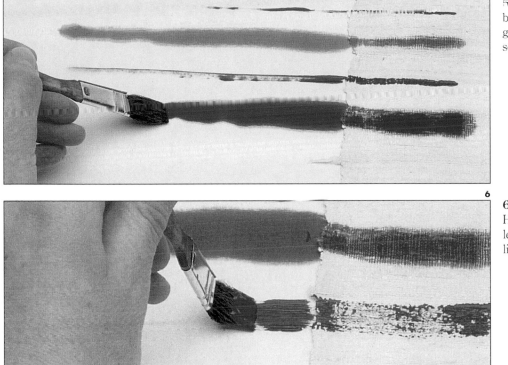

5 A soft, flat ½in. (1.5cm) brush and unthickened dye gives a flat unbroken line with some spreading.

6 The same brush used with Helizarin colour and binder leaves a rougher, more broken line.

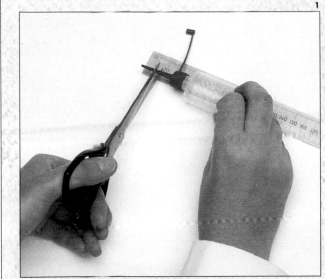

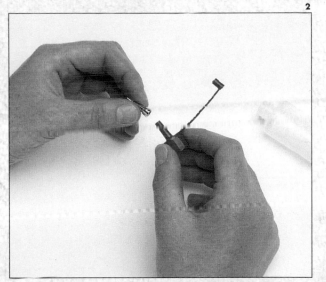

Using a Bottle and Nozzle

These useful bottles can be used for applying thickened dye or gutta. They are clean and easy to use and a handy way of applying linear marks.

Measure ½in. (17mm) from the tip of the plastic nozzle of the new bottle and snip off the end with a pair of sharp scissors *(1)*. Fit the metal tip over the end of the nozzle. Fill the bottle ⅔ full with medium to be used. Make sure the wire is inserted into the medium. Screw the nozzle with the metal tip on to the bottle *(2)* and it should then be ready to use.

BRUSH STROKES

7 Poly brushes, which are in fact made from foam rubber cut in a wedge shape and mounted on a handle, are available in a variety of sizes, and can be used flat or on their sides to give a variety of marks. They are very absorbent and so are appropriate for using with textile media.

8 Other, less obvious utensils can be used for applying colour to silk, depending on the mark you are trying to achieve. Here a plastic glue spreader *(a & b)* is used (see the Icon project, page 118, where metallic ready-to-use pigment is applied with a plastic glue spreader). You will probably find any number of things with which you can improvise: small pieces of card; small pieces of textured fabric such as corduroy or fur fabric; corrugated cardboard, etc. Very often only a small selection of brushes is required (see brushes page 34).

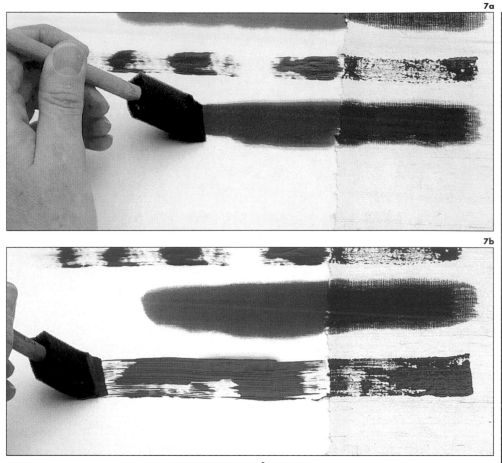

7a

7b

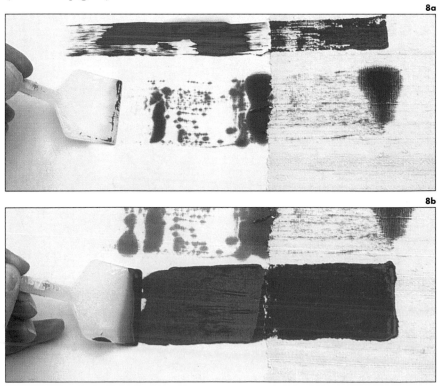

8a

8b

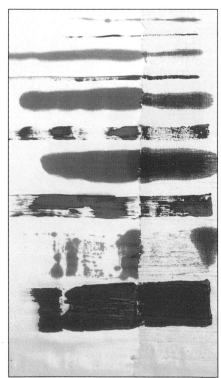

9a

9b

9c

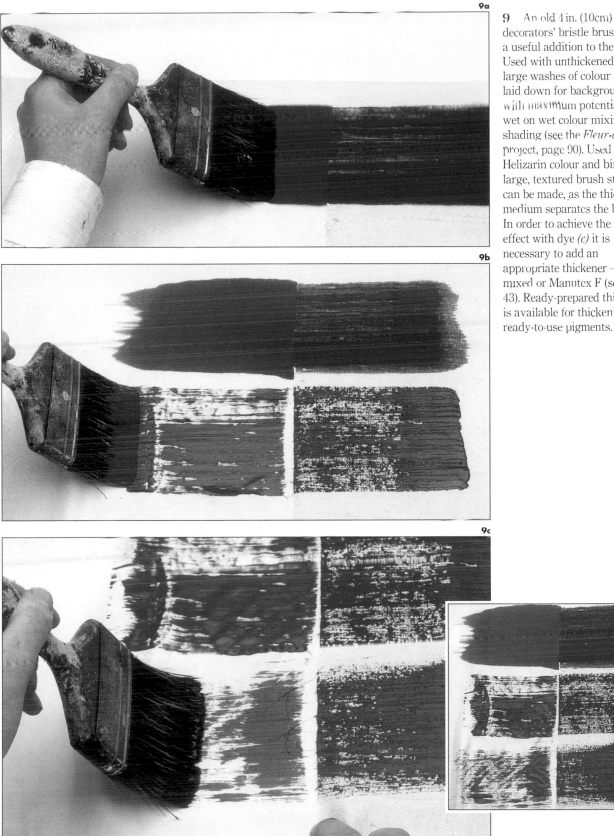

9 An old 4 in. (10cm) decorators' bristle brush can be a useful addition to the range. Used with unthickened dye *(a)*, large washes of colour can be laid down for backgrounds, with maximum potential for wet on wet colour mixing or shading (see the *Fleur-de Lys* project, page 90). Used with Helizarin colour and binder *(b)*, large, textured brush strokes can be made, as the thick medium separates the bristles. In order to achieve the same effect with dye *(c)* it is necessary to add an appropriate thickener – ready mixed or Manutex F (see page 43). Ready-prepared thickener is available for thickening ready-to-use pigments.

STEAMING

The main disadvantage of using dyes is that they remain susceptible to water until they have been steamed. All the projects in this book which use dyes are on small enough pieces of silk to be steamed in a domestic pressure cooker. For the really committed painter on silk, who wishes to produce large-scale pieces, a special textile steamer is required. These are very expensive and are therefore only worth acquiring if large-scale production is envisaged. Such steamers will steam between 16½-22 yards (15-20m) of silk at a time.

Steaming by Pressure Cooker

Pin the finished piece painted with dye to a clean piece of calico *(1)* at least 4 in. (10cm) larger than the silk on all sides. Make sure the silk is secured to the calico at the corners and about every 3 in. (7.5cm) all round.

Fold the calico over the silk at the foot and fold over again so that the painted silk is touching the calico where it is folded *(2)*. It is very important that none of the painted silk comes in to contact with itself, or any unpainted parts

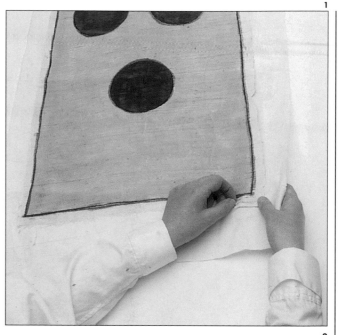

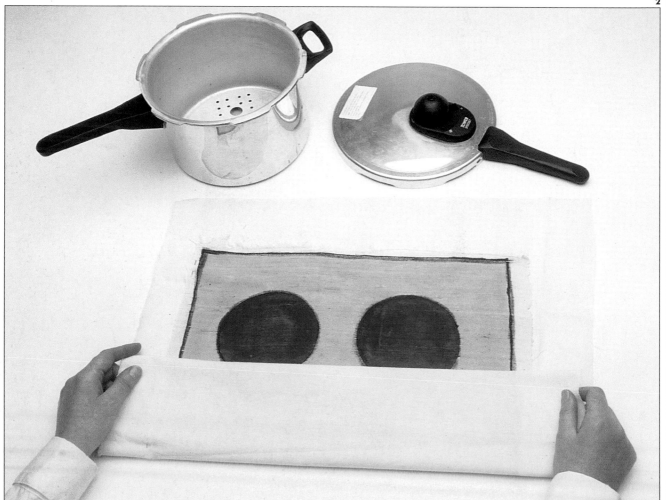

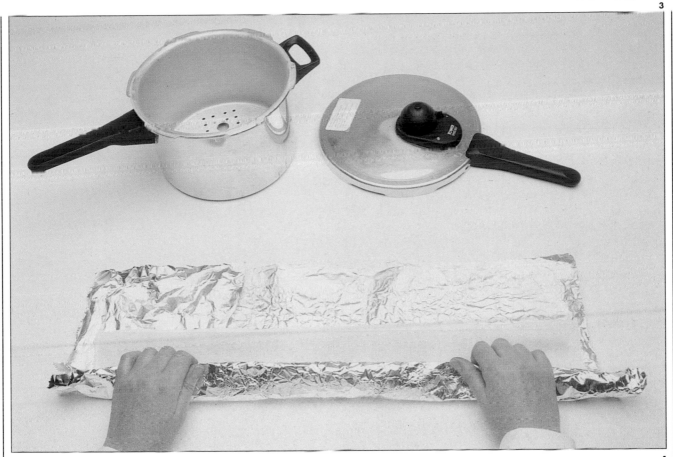

4

of the silk, as dye can get transferred during the steaming process. The calico will absorb any dye which is dampened during steaming before fixing is complete, stopping it from staining the piece. Repeat until the silk is completely rolled inside the calico and no longer visible.

Roll the calico and silk into a piece of aluminium foil *(3)* slightly wider than the calico. Partly crumple the ends of the foil over the ends of the calico roll, so that steam can enter and to prevent the possibility of condensation entering the roll and damaging the colour before it is fully fixed.

Place the trivet inside the pressure cooker *(4)* and add approximately ¾ in. (2cm) water. The parcel can be placed in the vegetable basket inside the pressure cooker or, as long as it is not in contact with the water, on the trivet if it will not fit in the vegetable basket. It is most important that the roll is not in contact with the water or it will become saturated and damaged before the colour is fixed.

Steam for 45 minutes on your pressure cooker's lowest setting. ***Check manufacturers' instructions for any variation on the quantity of water or pressure used***. Then rinse the silk in cold water (some colour may appear to wash out, but continue rinsing until the water is clear), then wash in warm, soapy water. Rinse, dry and iron on the wrong side.

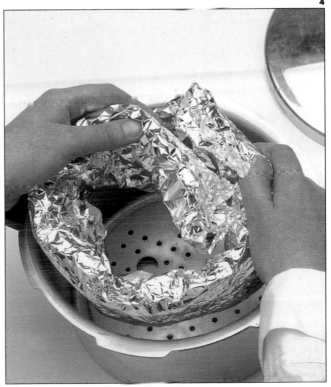

WET ON WET AND WET ON DRY

With dyes little difference is made painting wet on wet, or wet on dry, as unfixed dye colour is reactivated by being wetted after it is dry. Pigment colour (whether it is ready-to-use or colour mixed with binder), because it is fixed by dry heat, becomes more stable as it dries, so that different effects can be achieved by painting wet on dry from painting wet on wet. There are limitations to painting Helizarin colour and binder wet on dry, as the top layers will be inclined to wash off after fixing. This medium bonds better to the surface of fabric than to itself. Sometimes limitations such as these can be used to good effect when the result is appropriate to the subject. It is possible also to paint pigment wet on to a dry dyed background, so long as the dyed background has been fixed first (by steaming, see page 48). This method is used in the Red 'Pompeian' project on page 126.

Dyes

Yellow dye is painted wet on wet *(1)* on to a blue dye background. The colour blends into the blue to create a subtle green *(2)*.

Yellow dye is painted wet on dry *(3)* on to a blue dye background and, because the background has not been fixed, the blue is reactivated and behaves in much the same way as if it had been painted wet on wet *(4)*.

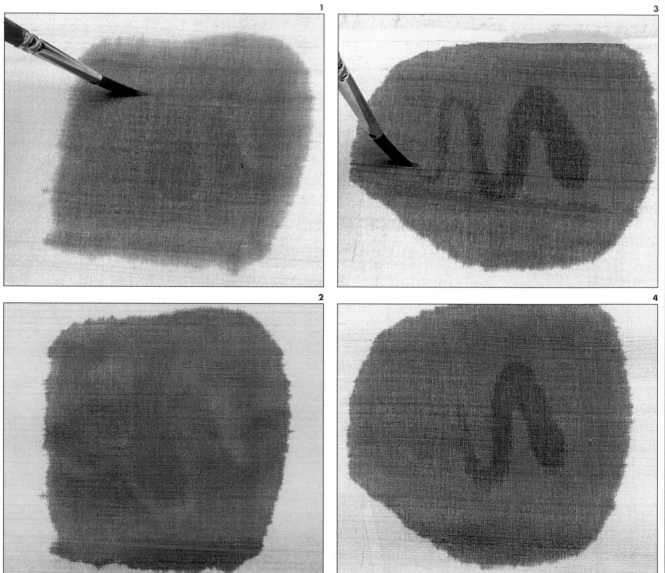

Pigments

Yellow Helizarin colour mixed with binder is painted wet on wet *(1)* onto a blue Helizarin pigment and binder background. The colours blend together to give a subtle green *(2)*.

Yellow Helizarin colour mixed with binder is painted wet on dry *(3)* on to a blue Helizarin colour and binder background. Because the blue background has become quite stable by being left to dry, the yellow shows up reasonably well. However, for a yellow which completely obliterates the blue background, the Helizarin colour is mixed into Bricoprint Opaque White T *(4)*. The final effect can be seen here *(5)*. For the best results when overpainting with Helizarin colour and binder wet on dry, it is generally advisable to use dye for the painted background. It is essential, however, that this is first fixed by steaming (see page 48) before the Helizarin colour and binder is overpainted. However, you may wish to experiment painting Helizarin colour and binder over Helizarin colour and binder dry backgrounds and notice the effects created by the removal of some of the overpainting during the washing-out process after fixing.

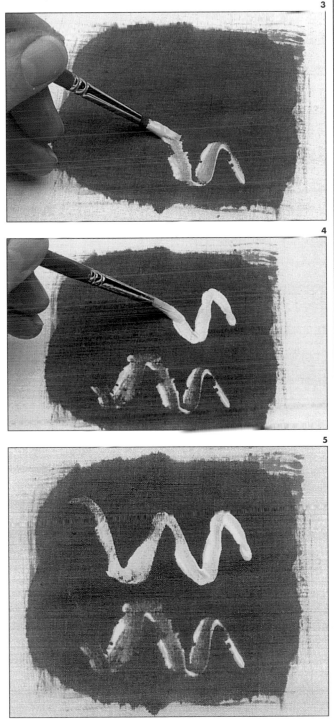

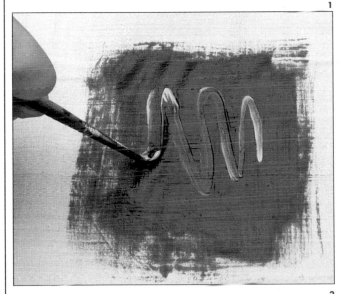

OTHER TECHNIQUES

Most of the techniques shown over the next few pages are demonstrated with Helizarin colour and binder. They work best with a viscous medium. If you wish to use dye or ready-to-use pigment, then it must be thickened with the appropriate thickener. Always wear rubber gloves if your hands will come into contact with the medium.

All the results of the various techniques will need to be fixed in the manner appropriate for the media to give an accurate record of how they will turn out. After fixing, rinse in cold water; wash in warm, soapy water; rinse, dry and iron on the wrong side.

Gutta

Batik-style effects can be created without using melted wax, but by using gutta instead. The great advantage of gutta is that it does not have to be heated and it does not leave a mark on the silk when it is removed after painting.

Gutta can be applied with any size of brush *(1)*, or with a container with a nozzle *(2)*. It is available clear, in colours and in metallics *(3)*. The gutta is first painted or drawn on the silk and left to dry. The gutta then acts as a resist and will stop colour from penetrating on to the cloth wherever it has been applied (N.B. optimum resistance is achieved on thin silk like habotai). Some penetration of colour occurs on thicker silks. It is advisable to do some test samples before embarking on a big piece. Paint over the dry gutta with colour (either thickened or unthickened). Leave to dry. Fix in the appropriate manner; rinse in cold water; wash in warm soapy water; rinse, dry, and iron on the wrong side. Clear gutta will wash out leaving the silk unpainted in the areas where the gutta has been applied. In the case of coloured or metallic gutta the appropriate effect will be left on the silk after fixing and washing. It will look clearer and brighter than if the colour had been applied first.

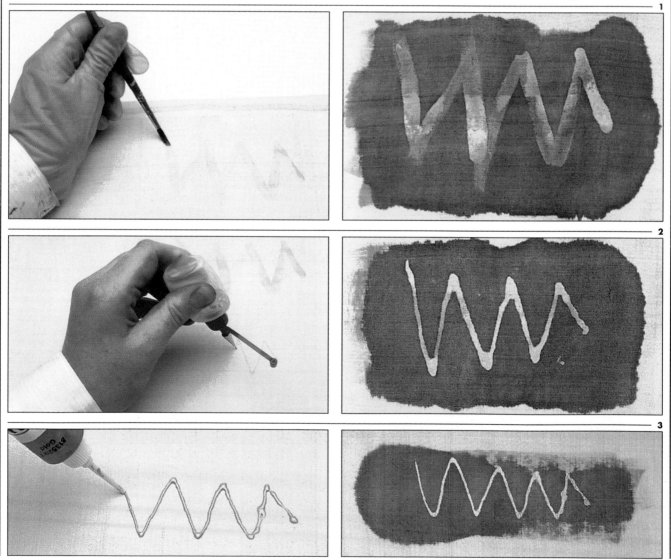

Primer

To prevent unthickened colour from spreading, a primer can be painted on the silk. Unlike primer used on canvas, this can be washed out once the textile media used for subsequent painting have been fixed in the appropriate way. The primer is inclined to discolour the silk slightly, so it is usually best to apply it over the whole area to be painted. It is useful for creating watercolour effects without the risk of the unthickened colour spreading and blending in an uncontrolled way. Paint the primer (Javana 'Aquarellgrund' is used here) on to the silk so that the whole area to be painted is covered. Leave to dry thoroughly. Here the primer has been painted in a strip to show how the colour painted over it is affected. By painting over the edge of the dry primer in one brush stroke, which falls partly on the primed surface and partly on the unprimed silk, it can be seen that the colour spreads more on the unprimed silk. Where the silk has been primed, the marks made with the colour are easier to control. Fix the colour in the appropriate manner. **Do not** wash the fabric in soapy water at this stage, as the primer will stiffen the silk if introduced to soap or detergent and become impossible to remove. Instead, soak the painted silk in plenty of hot water for half an hour. Rinse thoroughly. Wash in warm soapy water when you are confident all the primer is removed. Rinse, dry, and iron on the wrong side.

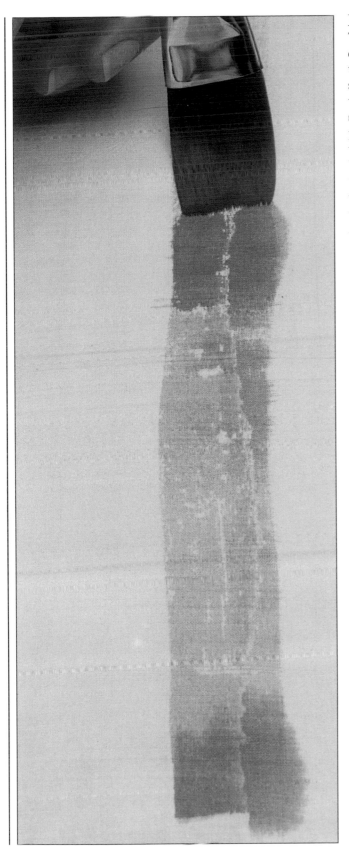

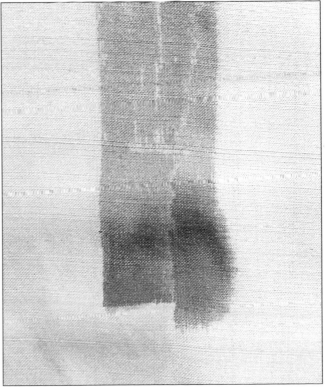

OTHER TECHNIQUES

Rolling

Colour can be applied with a roller directly onto the silk. Spread some thickened colour onto a piece of glass (ask the glass merchant to grind the edges when you have the glass cut, making it safe to handle). Roll lightly until the roller has an even coating of colour (1) and transfer the colour from the roller on to the cloth (2). The effect can be varied by rolling in different directions on to the silk.

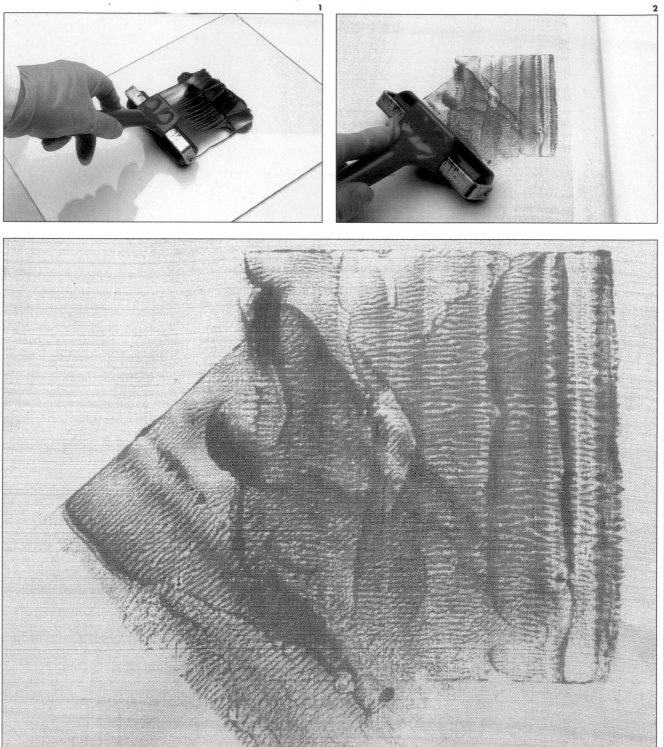

Sponging

Small pieces of sponge can be cut up, dipped into the colour, then dabbed on to the silk. Care must be taken not to saturate the sponge or the textured surface will become blurred and blobby.

Stippling

A stiff stippling brush, generally used for stencilling (see the *Fleur-de-Lys* project, page 90) can be used freehand to create a mottled effect (shading and blending can be introduced by using different colours or tones).

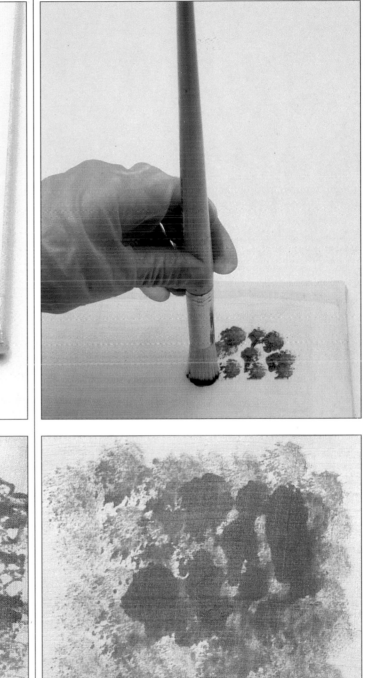

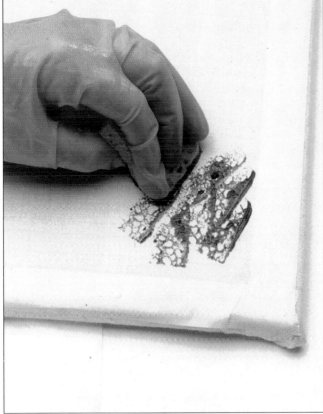

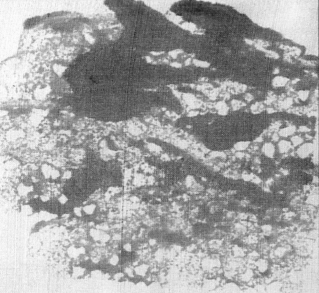

OTHER TECHNIQUES

Felt Tips

Felt tip pens specially designed for textile use are
extremely easy to use and the colours can be fixed by
ironing. A great deal of control can be exercised over
making precise, fine lines. The pens can also be used for
cross-hatching, freehand detail, or outlines, and used
alongside other textile media (see the 'Grotesque' project,
page 100).

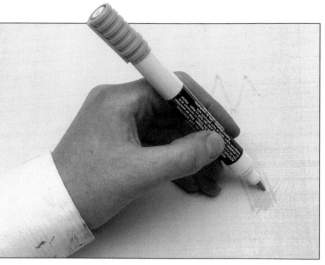

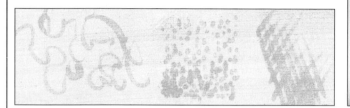

Effect Salts

Effect salt is generally used on dye or ready-to-use
pigment. The colour is painted and then the effect salt is
sprinkled on to it while the colour is still wet. The salt
draws up the dye, making the colour darker where the
crystals have come into contact with the wet dye and the
silk. The final effect is mottled. This technique works most
dramatically on fine silk with dye, but can be used to gain
varying effects on different silks. Ready-to-use pigment
can be used effectively, too. Effect salt is combined with a
number of other techniques to help give the look inspired
by aged paint when used on noile in the Red 'Pompeian'
project (see page 126).

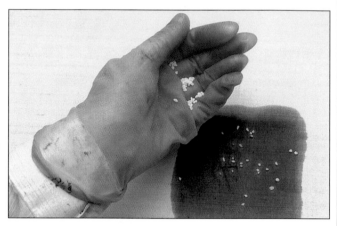

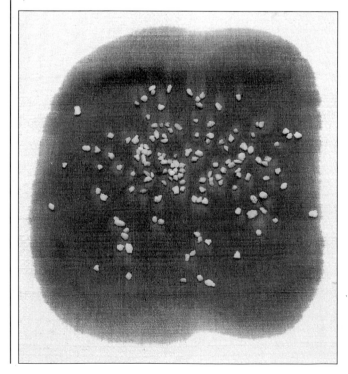

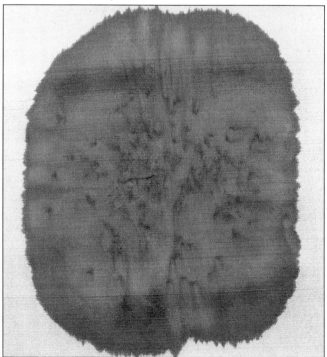

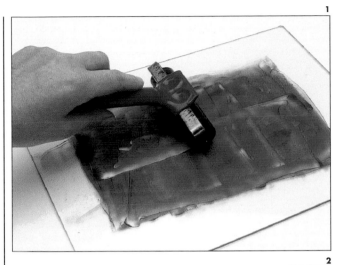

Monoprints

Simple printing methods can be used on silk by means of linocuts (see the Vase of Flowers project, page 82) or even using the humble potato, cut and then printed. An extremely simple and direct way of transferring spontaneous drawing on to silk is the monoprint. A little thickened colour (see page 43 for a guide to thickeners) is rolled on to a glass plate *(1)* the same size as the silk to be printed. Roll the colour out until it is roughly 2 in. (5cm) smaller all round than the piece of silk intended for printing. Draw into the wet colour *(2)* with a blunt utensil (the end of a paintbrush, for instance). When the drawing is complete, lay the silk over the colour and press down evenly all over *(3)*. Peel back the silk carefully *(4)*. The colour and drawing will have transferred on to the silk *(5)*.

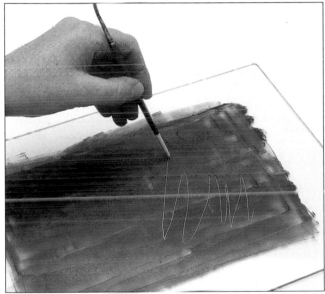

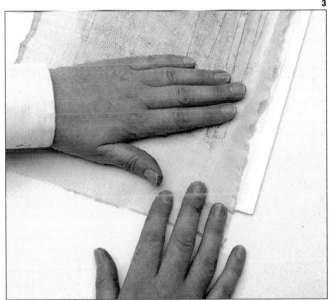

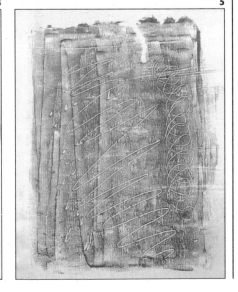

Chapter 4

Opaque and Translucent Colour

These two projects are based respectively on a page from a fourteenth-century book of arms and on a stained glass window. They demonstrate how three different textile media can be used to achieve different effects appropriate to the subject. Because marks made with dye and pigment are quite indelible it is wise to plan the composition of your work very carefully before beginning. Washing will reduce the intensity of colour which has not been fixed, but a stain will still remain on the fabric. Do not despair, even if you do make mistakes! These can be overpainted. The final result of your work might not be quite as you intended, but by building up colour in layers a wonderfully intense effect can be achieved. Colours can be mixed wet on wet to achieve maximum density and illusion of depth, or blotted with kitchen paper if they appear to be spreading out of control or are too dark.

It is very important to understand when and how to fix the various stages of colour when they have been applied. The following two projects are designed to show you how to plan compositions simply and directly. They also show the variations in the way in which dyes and pigments are absorbed by silk and by different types of silk, and how different they appear when they have been fixed.

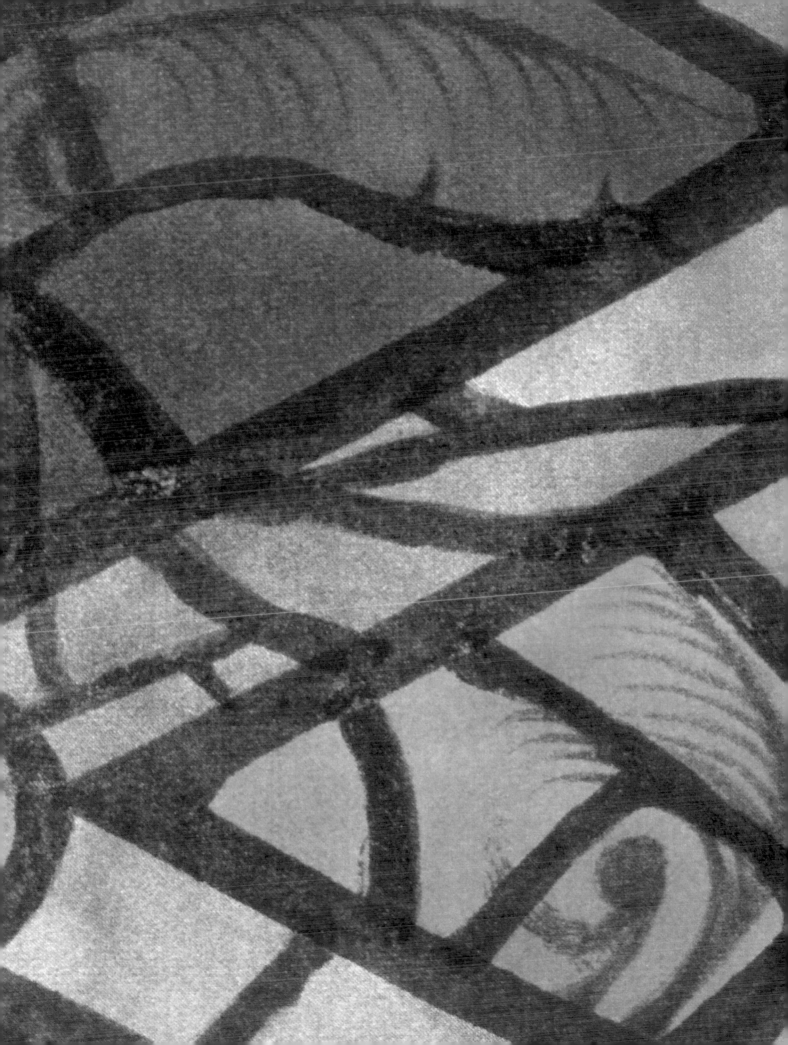

Heraldry

OPAQUE AND TRANSLUCENT COLOUR

Each of the three pieces in this project uses one of the three textile media (described in the Dyes and Pigments section of the Materials chapter). The blue panel uses pigment (Helizarin Colour) and Bricoprint Binder SF20. It shows how opaque it can be and how, through modifying the proper fixing process it can be used as a stain. The yellow and red panel with the blue border is painted with ready-to-use pigment (Javana Silk Paint) which is more translucent than pigment and binder, but equally easy to use, because it also requires dry heat for fixing. The yellow and red panel without a border uses dyes, which cannot be equalled for translucency and brilliance of colour while retaining the maximum sheen and character of the silk. Dyes must be fixed by steam. Three different types of silk have been chosen for the three panels to demonstrate the varying effects which can be achieved through choice of pigment or dye and different surfaces.

While just three panels have been used here, the project could be further developed using more of the shields in the reference as starting points. A group of small pieces laid out like those on the page of the book of arms shown below could be effective, or they could look very dramatic painted on a large scale as wall-hangings.

The blue piece demonstrates how the composition can be planned. The other two pieces demonstrate the different techniques required with the different media.

For each piece a rectangle of silk 27x19in. (68.5x48cm) is required, stretched and taped onto a padded board (see page 32) at least 29x21in. (73.5x53.5cm). You may find that you want to have all three pieces stretched on separate boards so that you can work on them together, filling in parts of one while another dries.

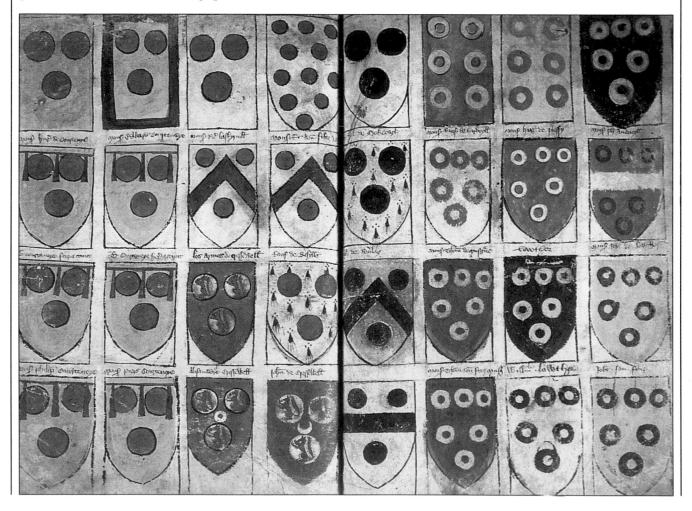

Blue Panel
(Helizarin pigment and binder on unbleached taffeta)

1   Draw a rectangle 24x16in. (61x40.5cm) using a 2B pencil and a ruler on to stretched silk. Apply the pencil lightly so that the marks will be camouflaged by the black lines drawn on top of them later. If you press too hard the pencil will catch on the silk.

2   Using black lining paint in a tube with a nozzle draw straight over the line. This line will not be as rigid as if you drew it using a ruler but it allows you to make a very straight line which appears to be quite freehand. Leave the gutta to dry; it takes quite a long while, so be patient or you will smudge it.

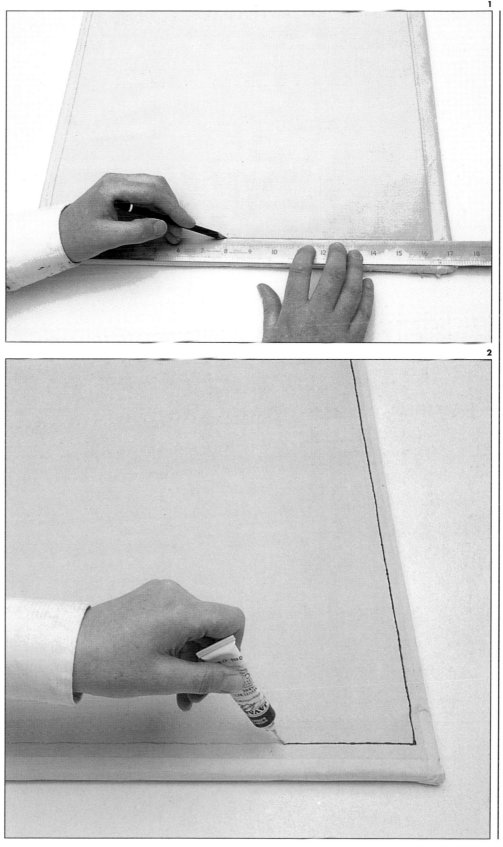

OPAQUE AND TRANSLUCENT COLOUR / HERALDRY

3 To make the large circular shapes use any conveniently sized circular shape to hand. Here a roll of masking tape provides the shape, drawn with a 2B pencil. You could use a saucer instead, or, if you choose to develop the projects on a larger scale later, a plate makes a very handy model.

4 A small container of stencil creme is used to provide the shape for the small, inner circles, still drawn with a 2B pencil.

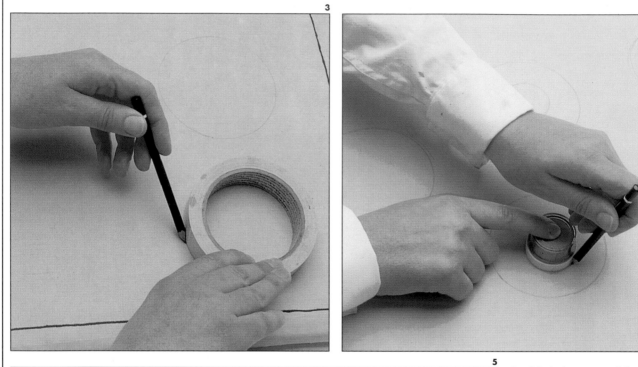

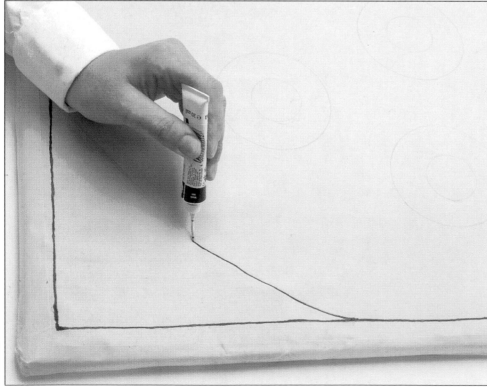

5 Mark the centre of the lower horizontal line of the rectangle with the pencil. On one vertical side of the rectangle measure 9 in. (23 cm) up from the lower corner and mark. Repeat on the other side. Using the pencil freehand, draw a curving line to join the marks on the sides with the mark at the centre of the lower line to make the lower part of the shield shape. Go over this line with black lining paint in a tube.

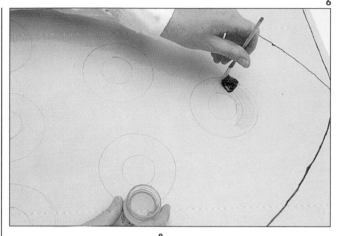

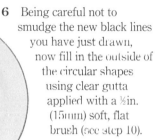

6 Being careful not to smudge the new black lines you have just drawn, now fill in the outside of the circular shapes using clear gutta applied with a ½in. (15mm) soft, flat brush (see step 10).

7 When the gutta is completely dry, iron the black lines and clear gutta painted circles to ensure they are thoroughly fixed and will not allow colour to penetrate on to the silk where it is not wanted.

8 Mix Helizarin Blue RT into Bricoprint Binder SF20 in an enamel dish. Build up the amount of colour drop by drop until the required shade is achieved (as shown in the illustration), mixing thoroughly until there are no traces of white left in the mixture (see page 42).

9 Using a 2½in. (6cm) flat, soft brush paint the blue pigment on the shield. The gutta on the circles will resist the colour so you can paint quite roughly around them. The colour is applied quite unevenly to mimic the effect in the original book of arms.

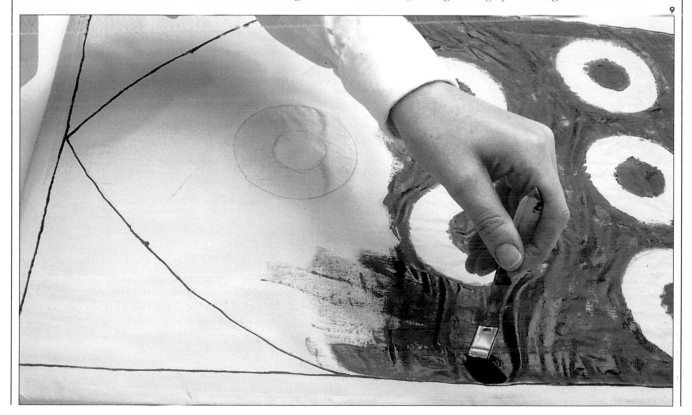

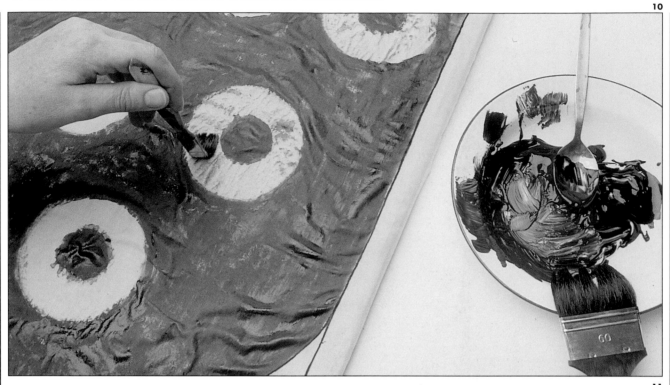

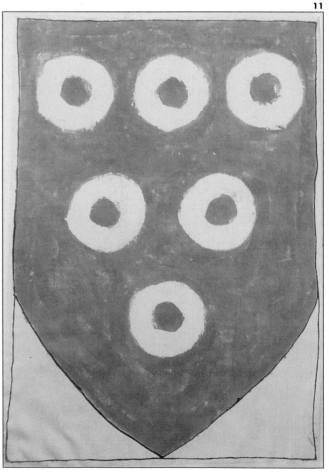

10 If you have painted the gutta on the circles quite thickly at step 6 you can safely paint straight over them with the pigment mixture. You might choose to experiment with the amount of gutta applied in step 6 and the amount of blue pigment painted over them at this stage. Where the gutta is painted it will resist the pigment and where the silk is left bare the blue will remain painted on the silk after washing. Leave the piece to dry. It will now look rather dark and bright, but still rather heavy and thick with the opaque pigment.

11 When the piece is completely dry, wash it thoroughly in warm soapy water making sure that you are wearing rubber gloves. Usually you would have fixed the pigment with dry heat before this stage, but this method allows you to paint the thick pigment over large areas and use it as a stain, thus removing the rather heavy appearance observed at the end of step 10. Rinse, dry, and iron on the wrong side, and you will see a much more subtle effect emerge.

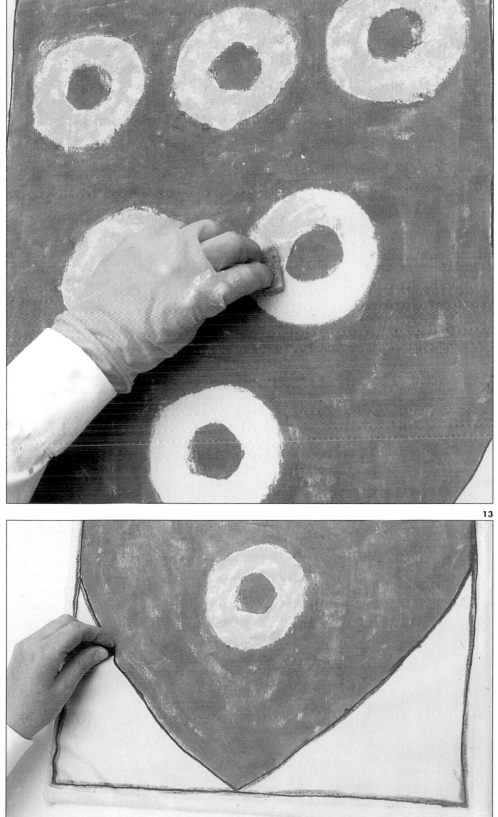

12 Mix a pale yellow, using Bricoprint Binder SF20 and Helizarin Yellow G. Only very small amounts of binder and colour are needed (about two teaspoonsfuls of binder and the smallest drop of colour). Wearing rubber gloves, apply the yellow to the circles, using a small piece of cut-up sponge and a soft padding motion. Do not put too much pigment on the sponge.

13 Finally apply black wax crayon specially made for textile use over the black lines. Even the specially made wax crayons do not show up very well on silk if used on their own, but in conjunction with the solid black lining paint the desired effect is achieved. The wax gives a softer appearance to the black lines more like the rough, hand-drawn quality of the lines in the original reference book. Iron on the wrong side for three minutes on the cotton setting. Wash in warm, soapy water; rinse, dry, and iron on the wrong side.

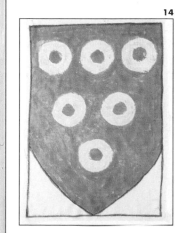

14 The finished piece. I conclude all three pieces at the end of the project.

Yellow and Red Panel with Blue Border
(ready to use pigments on white taffeta)

1   Using a 2½in. (6cm) soft, flat brush paint the entire area of silk with textile primer. Javana 'Aquarellgrund' watercolour primer allows the ready-to-use pigment to be painted on directly without any thickener. Spreading or 'bleeding' and the risk of dark edges of colour are minimized. Allow to dry thoroughly.

2   Draw up a rectangle first with a 2B pencil and then with black lining paint, following steps 1 and 2 for the blue piece. When the black lines are thoroughly dry, using the width of a ruler as a guide, draw a rectangle 1in. (2.5cm) inside the first rectangle, first with pencil and then with black lining paint, to make the border.

3   The circles are traced directly around a circular object, using black lining paint in a tube. However, take care when lifting the shape after the circle is complete, as the lining paint is very sticky and easily smudged. Leave to dry completely and then iron.

4   Maize Yellow (8192) Javana silk paint is used with a flat 1in. (2.5cm) brush for painting the background around the circles and the narrow parts of the composition near the border. You can use a larger brush for the areas which are not so confined. Although the primer stops the colour from running too much, as does the black lining paint, take care not to use the brush too close to the outlines when it is fully loaded with dye to avoid it spreading over the edges.

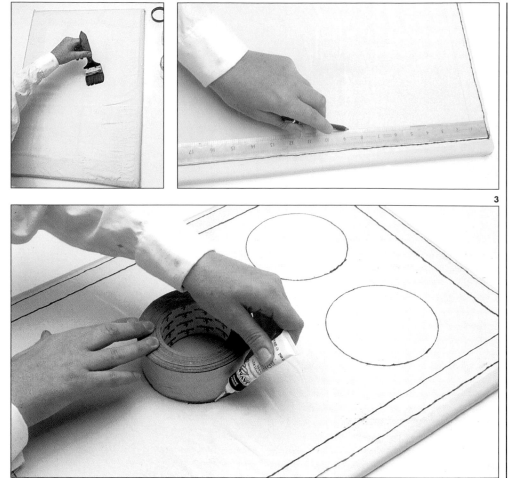

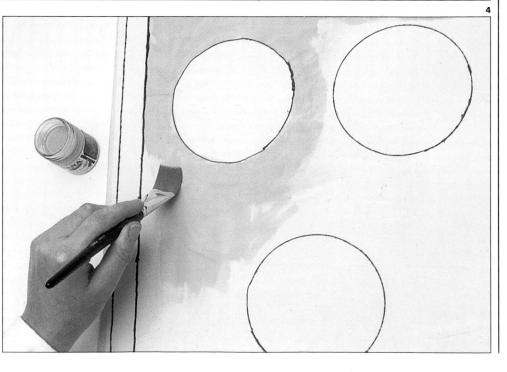

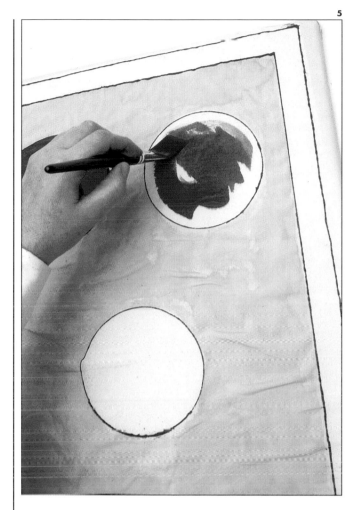

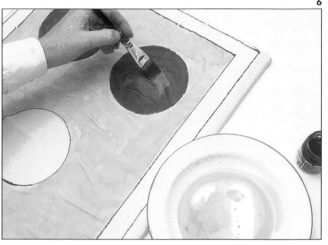

5 Next, fill the circles with Cherry Red (8194) Javana silk paint, taking care to start in the centre of the circles and work outwards to avoid blurring the edges. The colour here is applied in quite a solid way, but you might like to experiment with brush strokes, perhaps leaving more of the background silk showing.

6 Maize Yellow is mixed into the red while this is still wet, again starting in the centre and working outwards.

7 When the yellow and red are completely dry, the blue border is filled in with the 1in. (2.5cm) brush. When this is thoroughly dry, draw black wax crayon over the black lines, as in step 14 of the blue project. Iron for three minutes on the wrong side on the cotton setting. Soak for half an hour in hot water to remove the primer.

Do not use soap or detergent at this stage, as it makes the primer go very stiff and then it is impossible to remove from the silk.

Then wash, rinse, dry, and iron on the wrong side.

8 Again the finished piece is discussed in more detail at the end of the project.

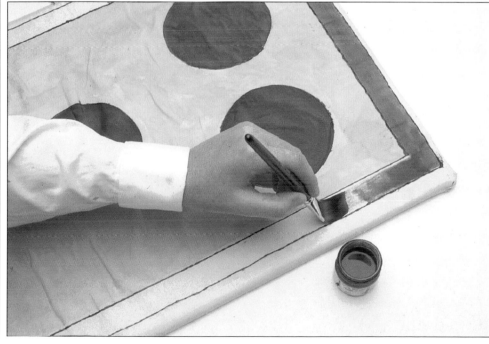

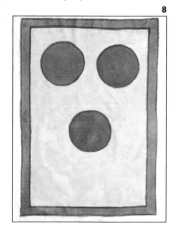

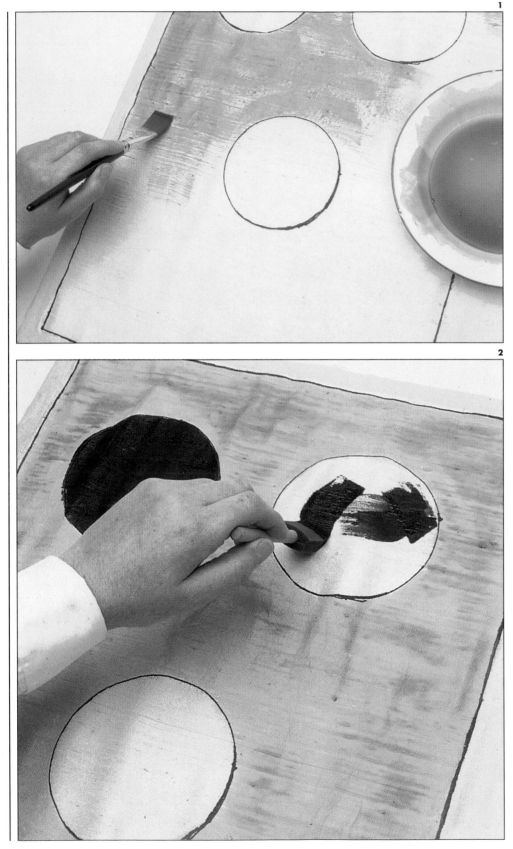

Yellow and Red Panel
(dyes on douppion)

1 The outside rectangle is drawn up following steps 1 and 2 for the blue piece. The circles are then made by repeating step 3 of the previous project. Dupont Jaune de Chrome (2000) is mixed with Manutex F (see page 43) so that it can be painted on the silk without spreading, using a 1in. (2.5cm) flat brush.

2 Using the same brush or a ½in. (1.5cm) soft brush, paint Dupont Rubis (2005) mixed with Manutex F on to the three circles, starting with a loaded brush in the middle and carefully working outwards to the edge of the circle. When the piece is thoroughly dry, steam it according to the instructions on page 48. Rinse in cold water. Wash in warm soapy water, rinse, dry, and iron on the wrong side. Re-stretch the silk on the board and apply black wax crayon lines over the black lining paint lines following step 14 for the blue piece. Iron on the wrong side for three minutes on cotton setting.

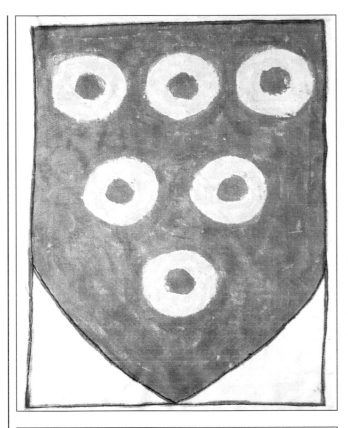

Conclusion

You have now tried the three main methods of painting on silk. Understanding the different properties of the media and how to fix them are the most important lessons. You are now equipped with experience which will help you to make the correct decisions about which dyes and silk to use when developing your own ideas in the future. You can now see that the dyes give brilliance and sheen, and the Helizarin colour and binder, even when washed out without proper fixing, is much more matte and textural, while the ready to use pigments give an effect somewhere between the two.

You may now be developing preferences for different media or considering ways you might develop this project, building on the experience you have gained.

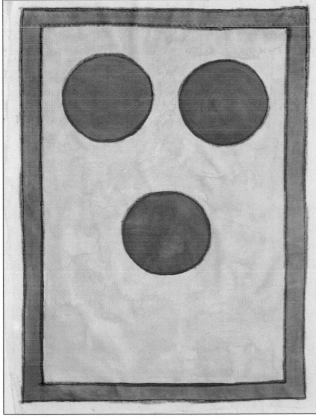

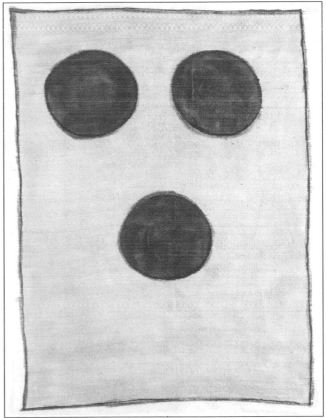

Stained Glass

OPAQUE AND TRANSLUCENT COLOUR

In this project opaque black pigment (Helizarin Black and Bricoprint Binder – you could use black lining paint) is used to represent the solid nature of the lead in the stained-glass window. It contrasts strongly with the vivid translucent colour obtainable with dye. Mixed wet on wet, the dye provides intense tones and depth of colour through repeated washes to represent the glass. The black pigment is not only opaque but also, when fixed (ironed) before the application of the dye, acts to some extent as a barrier to prevent the dye from spreading when wet. This allows you to use the dye like watercolour.

Take care not to overload the brush with dye, otherwise the colours will seep across the black 'leading'. If this happens, you should soak up the colour quickly with kitchen towel to avoid further spreading. The areas where the spreading has occurred should then be worked over with a little compatible colour. Sometimes these kind of mistakes can lead to exciting discoveries about varying colours. While the finished piece might end up less bright than you intended, you may well have gained new insights into colour mixing.

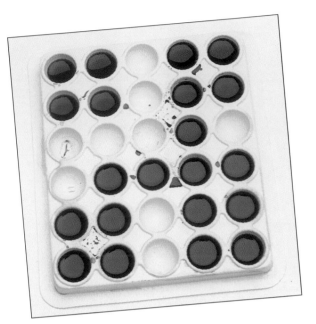

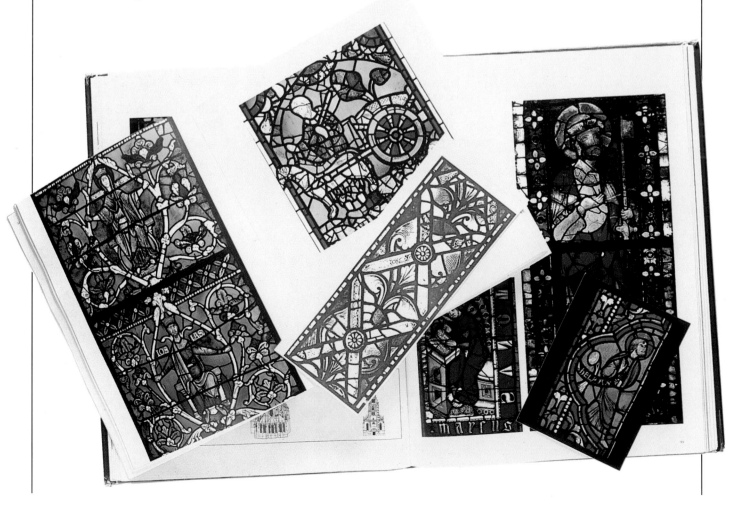

1 On a previously padded board (see page 32) measuring not less than 28x20 in. (71x51cm) stretch a piece of white taffeta measuring 25x17 in. (63.5x43cm). Using 1in. (2.5cm) or 2 in. (5cm) masking tape, mask the edges so that a neat rectangle 23x15 in. (58.5x38cm) remains clear in the centre. Do not leave any gaps in the masking tape. On the right-hand, vertical side of the rectangle, leaving an approximately ½ in. (1cm) gap inside the masking tape you have just laid down, position another piece of 1in. (2.5cm) masking tape parallel with the first and press down firmly (see step 5). Repeat on the left hand side.

2 Using a small soft, flat, tapered no. 8 brush and black Helizarin colour mixed into Bricoprint Binder SF20 (see page 42), paint in the gaps between the two sets of masking tape, making a black ½ in. (1cm) wide vertical line down each side. You can paint this quite rapidly as the masking tape ensures the lines will be clean and straight, but you must make sure that it has been pressed firmly down along the edges.

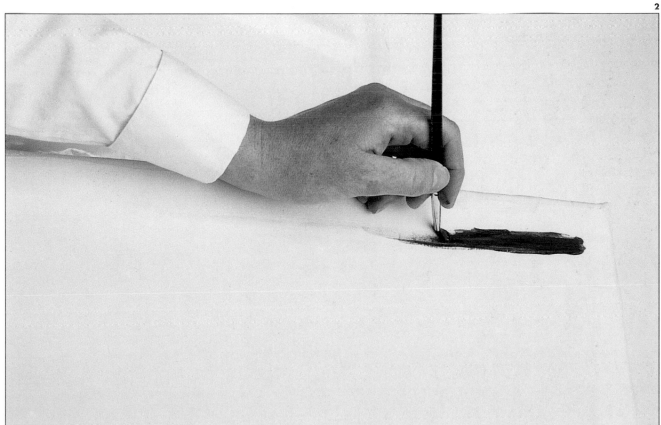

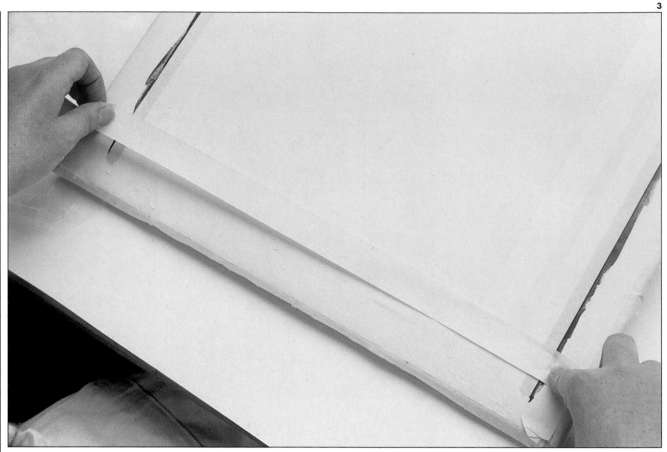

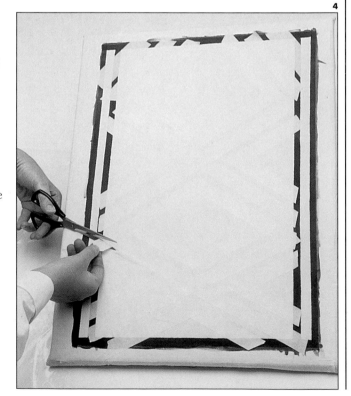

3 When the two black lines are thoroughly dry, lift the tape and discard. On the right-hand side, lay down 1in. (2.5cm) masking tape on top of the black line, covering approximately ½in. (1cm) of it. Approximately ½in. (1cm) towards the centre lay down another piece of 1in. (2.5cm) masking tape, parallel with this one, and press down firmly. Repeat on the other side. On the lower, horizontal side of the rectangle lay down 1in. (2.5cm) masking tape leaving approximately ½in. (1cm) gap. Repeat on the top, horizontal line. Lift the ends of the tape where they cross one another and interfere with the straight lines and snip neatly with a pair of scissors (see step 4). Paint the gaps with the black pigment mixture as in step 2.

4 Make the three cross shapes with 1in. (2.5cm) masking tape. This should be arranged so that you can paint in approximately ½in. (1cm) lines. (The photograph in step 9 can be used as a guide for placing the crosses; do not worry if they are a bit unevenly spaced. It would be very difficult to copy the original exactly.) Use scissors to snip where the masking tape overlaps.

5 Make sure that you press all the edges down very firmly before you start to paint so that the pigment will not seep under the edges of the tape, leaving neat edges to the lines. Paint as in step 2 and leave to dry.

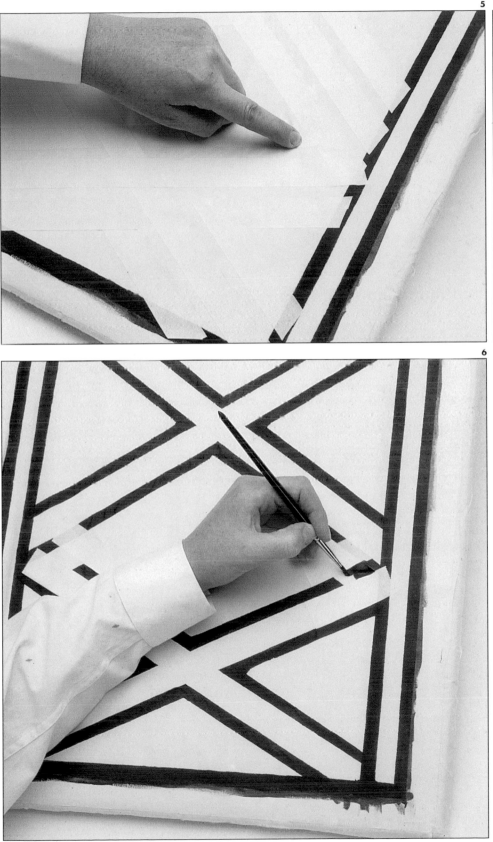

6 When the painting is completely dry and you have removed the masking tape, you may find that you have missed some parts of the ends of the lines because the masking tape has obscured them. Cut small pieces of tape to fit the missing parts and arrange them as necessary, so that you can continue the lines with the black and complete the composition.

7 Now apply the irregular and circular lines of the 'leaded' patterns using freehand lines. You can use the same soft, flat, tapered no. 8 brush, employing the flat side for the broader lines. Start at the top of the composition and work down, so that you don't smudge the wet pigment as you work.

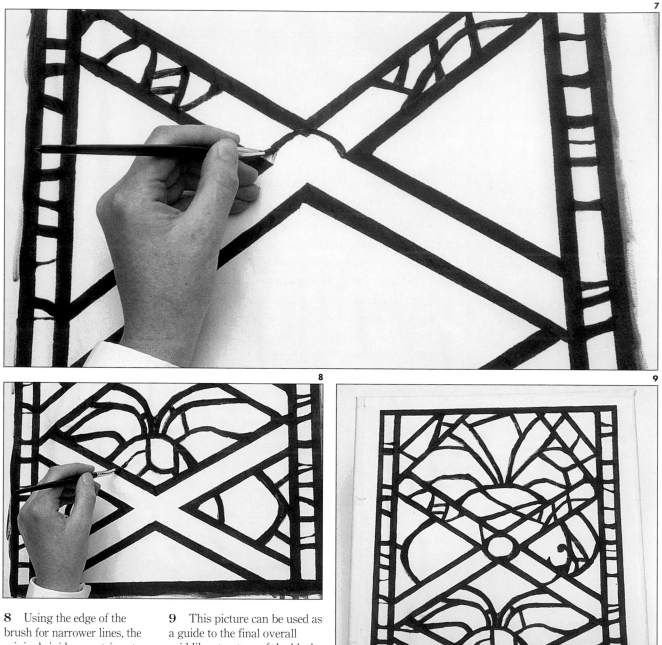

8 Using the edge of the brush for narrower lines, the original rigid geometric nature of the composition now begins to take on a more fluid appearance.

9 This picture can be used as a guide to the final overall grid-like structure of the black 'leading'. Once the basic structure has been laid down with masking tape and painted, then the freehand lines can be improvised quite rapidly to provide a lively counterpart to the bold forms created by the cross shapes and vertical lines.

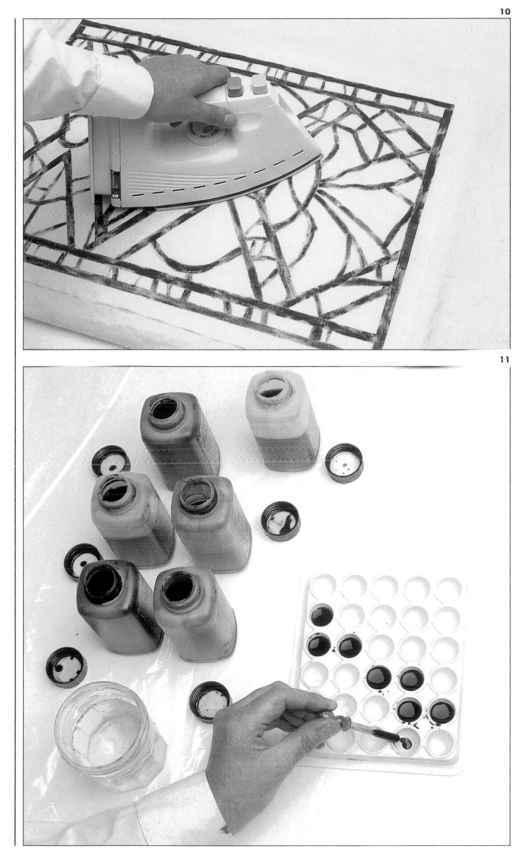

10 Leave the black pigment to dry thoroughly (preferably overnight). Remove the silk from the board and iron on the reverse side for three minutes on the cotton setting.

This step is extremely important. It fixes the black pigment lines so that they will help to prevent the dyes (which are applied next) from spreading.

11 Using an eye dropper, measure small amounts of dye into a palette with very small containers. The eye dropper is invaluable for transferring small amounts of dye out of the bottles without making a terrible mess. Wash the eye dropper thoroughly with water between measuring out each colour.

12 It is advisable to start with the yellow – Dupont Jaune de Chrome (2000) – using a very clean brush as it is the lightest colour and is most liable to be tainted by other colours. Because the dyes are so concentrated, you must wash brushes extremely thoroughly. Even the residues of dye on the brush can affect other colours which are used later.

Start in the centre of the spaces where the colour is to be applied and work outwards, so that only a little colour is left on the brush when it gets close to the black outlines. It is possible to apply most of the colour in the centre of each space with a loaded brush and then allow it to seep outwards. A soft no. 12 brush is used.

13 For the red I used Dupont Rubis (2005) and Rose (2006), mixed together and shaded wet on wet. Wash the brushes thoroughly between colours where purity of colour is required, or allow the residual colour already on the brush to form the basis of the next colour to be painted. The green on the left, for example, was made with Dupont Côte d'Azur (2010) and Jaune de Chrome (2000) and applied while the brush still had some of the red mixture on it. This has dulled the intensity of the green.

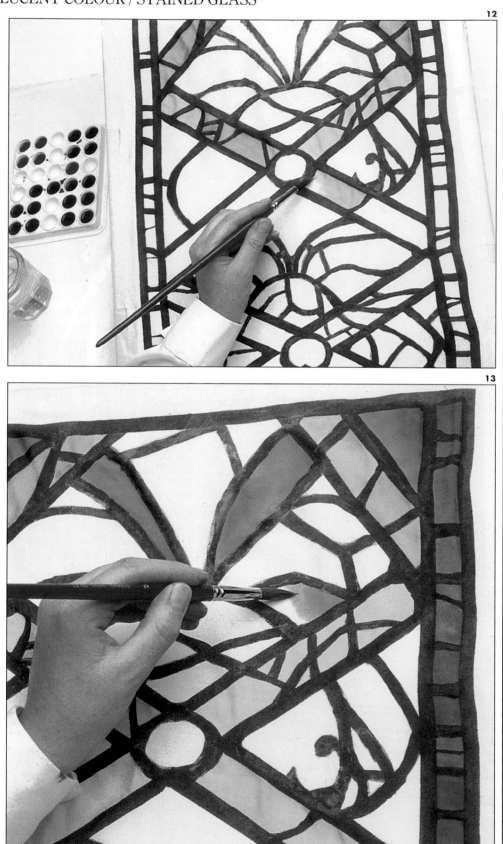

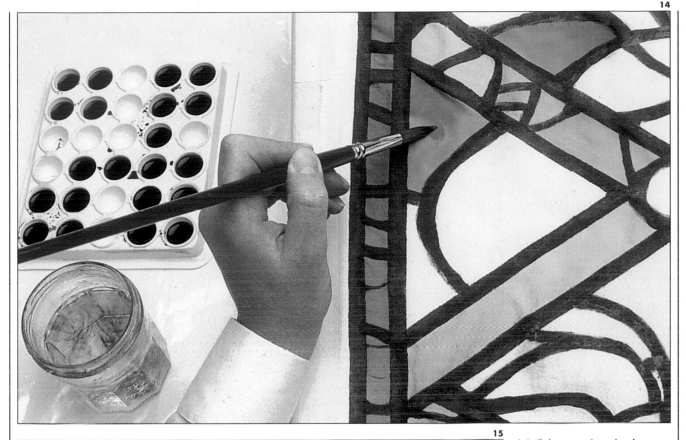

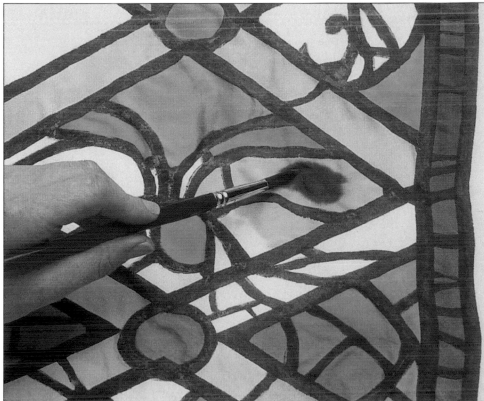

14 Colour can be mixed wet on wet to give shades of tone or to mix colour.

15 Be extra careful when working wet on wet not to flood the silk and allow the colours to spread across the black lines. If this does happen, build on your mistakes to create rich, dark colours like this red. This was created by working over a yellow which had also absorbed some turquoise.

16 This illustration can be used as a guide for the overall layout of colours if you wish.

17 When you have applied all the colours, leave them to dry completely. Using a very fine, soft 00 brush and Dupont Noir Concentré (2019), fill in the detail of the patterns on the coloured 'glass' parts. The translucent black dye contrasts with the black opaque pigment and gives depth, as well as detail, to the whole composition. Be careful not to put too much dye on to this little brush, so that the marks you make remain light and feathery. When all the colour is dry, steam following the instructions on page 48. Wash in warm, soapy water; rinse, dry, and iron on the wrong side.

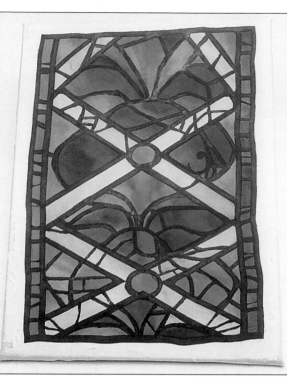

18 If you have had trouble controlling the colours and the finished piece has not turned out quite as you anticipated, do not worry. You have probably discovered some unexpected colour combinations and hopefully have been inspired by these to experiment further with dyes. If you have found the formal arrangement of masking areas to apply the black pigment too complicated you might like to experiment, using just the dyes as washes. You can then create compositions with brilliant, powerful colour, almost as if you were using watercolour.

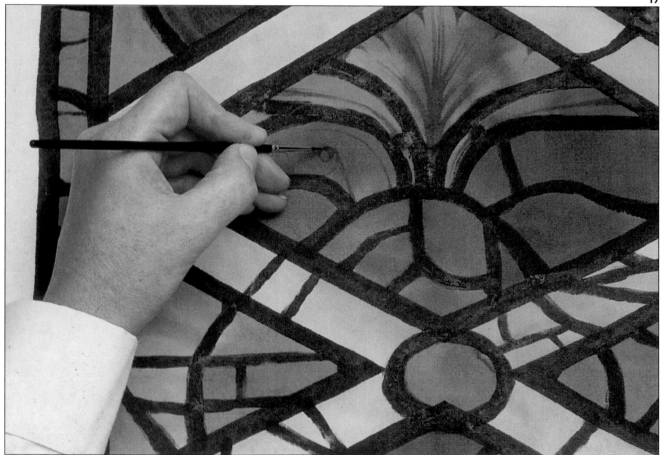

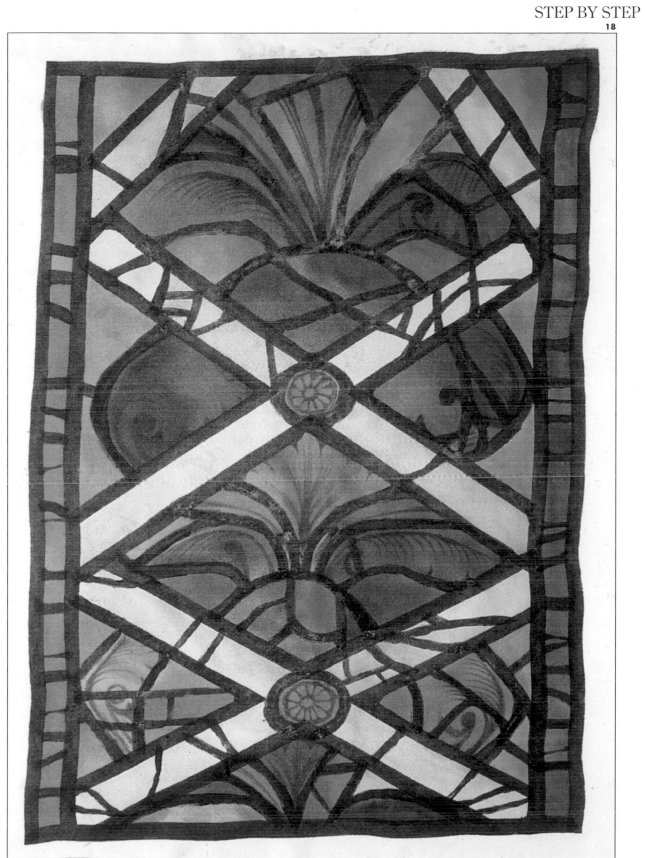

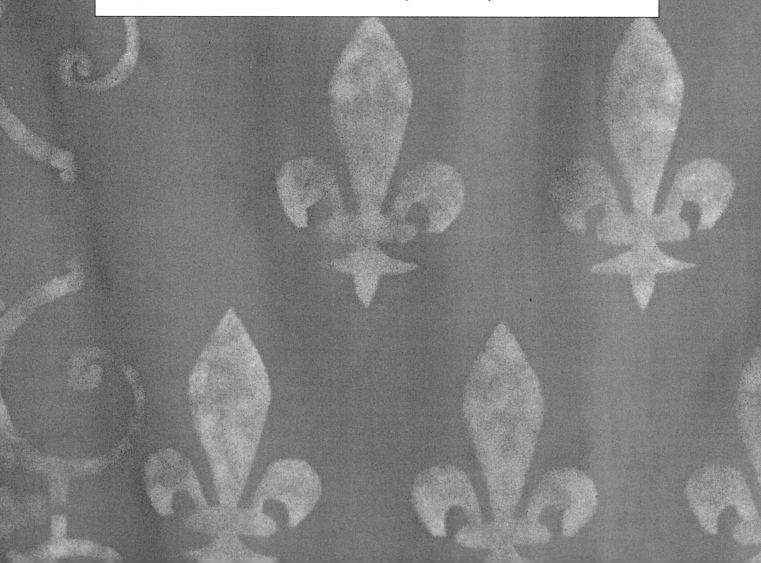

Chapter 5
Linocuts & Stencils

The planning of a composition is, as we have already seen, a very important consideration when painting on silk. New means of drawing, too, need to be developed, which take into account the way the fabric behaves. It can be quite daunting at first when all the media you are using seem to misbehave. Practice is, of course, the answer but, if you are a beginner and perhaps not completely confident about your drawing, then using other means to put shape and line down on the silk in a very direct way can be a good starting point for building up confidence.

If you really do have a problem with your drawing, then stencils and linocuts can transform your most timid first steps. Very often it is just lack of confidence which is the problem. In the 'vase of flowers' project an enlargement was made from the original reference on a photocopier and then traced on to lino. The lino-cutting techniques, which require vigorous gouging, give the rather characterless lines of the tracing a brand new life. The linocut was then used as a basis for overpainting to produce the soft, rather pastel-like effect of the finished painting.

The *'fleur-de-lys'* project deliberately uses a very simple motif to show how choice of colour and medium can give bold, grand effects without complicated techniques.

Vase of Flowers

LINOCUTS AND STENCILS

The vase of flowers design was enlarged by photocopying (up to A3 size) from a postcard of a *scagliola* table in the Victoria and Albert Museum, London. The vase was traced from the photocopy (although it could have been drawn on to the lino freehand) and transferred on to the lino. A rough douppion silk has been used, which gives texture to the colour where it is applied, giving the final piece a rather soft appearance.

The linocut was made as a 'negative'. That is, the main parts of the drawing were cut out so that they could be coloured in on the silk with a brush. The background was left uncut so that it could receive the dye from the roller and print on to the silk, thus laying down the base for the black background.

Dupont dye mixed with thickener was chosen for the black background of the lino print as it represents quite a large proportion of the piece and dyes interfere least with the surface qualities of the cloth. After this had been fixed by steaming, further depth was added to the background with ready-to-use pigment, which was also used for the details of the flowers and vase. Dyes mixed with thickener can be used for the details for even more glowing colours, but these need to be fixed by steaming after application.

Use a piece of douppion 18x14 in. (45.5x35.5cm) taped to a previously padded board no smaller than 22x18 in. (56x45.5cm) (see page 32).

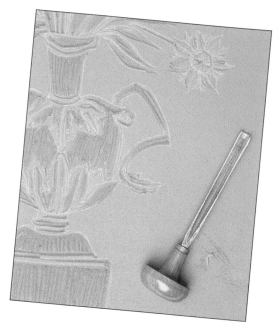

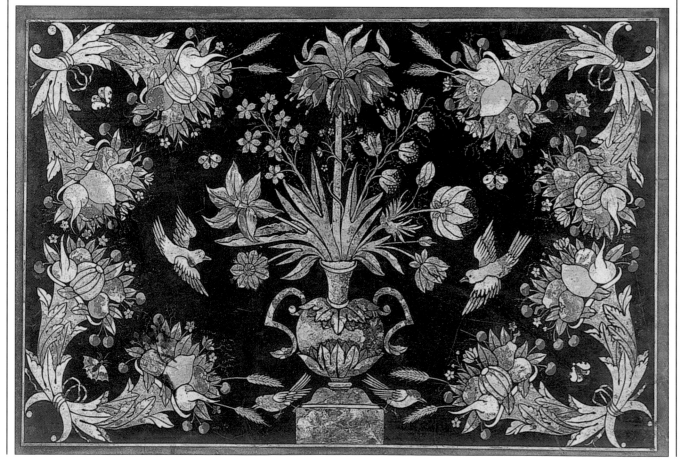

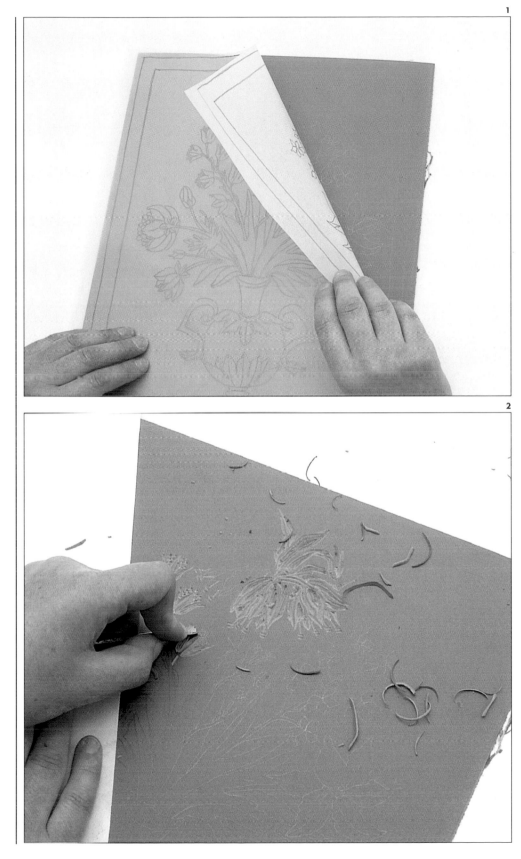

1 Enlarge the image on the photocopier to A3 size. Trace the main elements of the vase and flowers with a 2B pencil. Draw a rectangular border round the edge of the tracing to measure 15x10 in. (31x25.5cm). Turn the tracing paper over and, using an HB pencil, transfer the drawing on to a piece of lino roughly 16x12 in. (40.5x30.5cm). Place the tracing slightly to one side on the lino so that you can cut a band down one edge to make it easier to pick up when printing. At each stage of the tracing it is advisable to secure the tracing at the corners with small pieces of masking tape. The tracing will be quite faint on the lino, so go over it again with a 2B pencil.

2 Put a piece of kitchen towel under your hand where it touches the block so that you do not smudge the drawing as you cut. Different elements of the picture require different types of gouging and this is what gives the drawing its own character. Short, sharp cuts are made for the details of the flowers.

Always keep your free hand ***behind*** the hand which holds the cutting tool and cut away from you. ***never*** cut towards you.

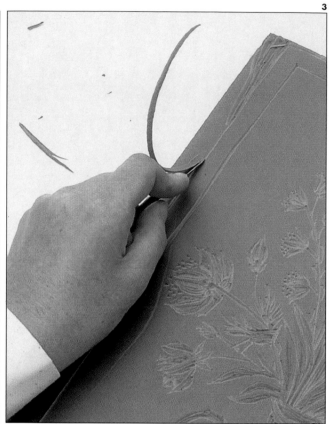

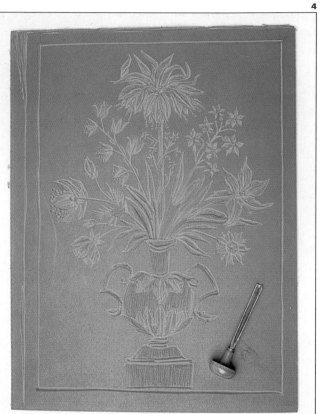

3 A long, smooth gouge is made along the rectangular border to give a freehand look to the outline.

4 The finished lino-block shows how the final effect will look. Note how I have started to cut away a section down the left-hand side, along the outside of the border, to make the turning over and placing on the silk easier during printing.

5 The printing from the block must be done with thickened colour. For this project, black Dupont dye (Noir Concentré 2019) was used, mixed with ready-to-use thickener. You could use Manutex F to thicken the dye (see page 43).

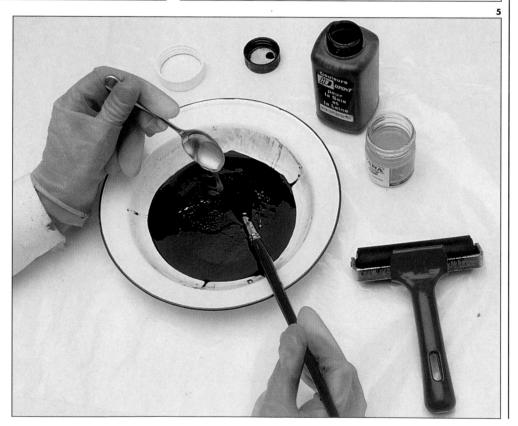

6 On a piece of glass measuring approximately 10x8 in. (25.5x20.5cm) (ask your glass merchant to grind the edges when it is cut for you, making it safe to handle) spread the thickened dye mixture in a strip about ½ in. (1.5cm) by the width of your roller. Roll the mixture backwards and forwards on the roller so that the roller is evenly coated; only a relatively light touch is required.

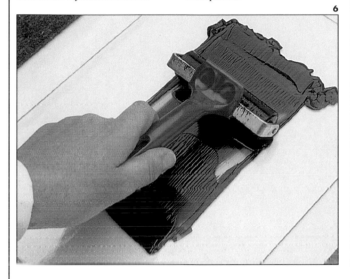

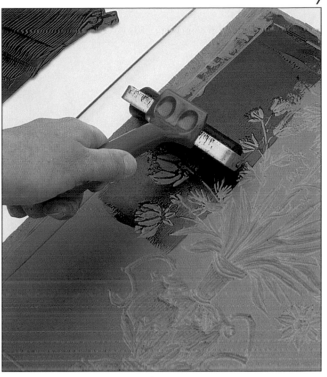

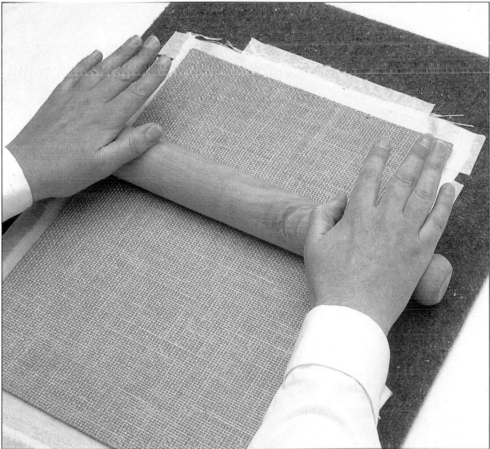

7 Using an even backwards and forwards motion coat the lino-block with a thick layer of the black dye mixture. You may find that you get better results if you first paint the cut lino across its entire surface with primer to seal it, so that the dye does not get absorbed by the lino. Leave the primer to dry thoroughly before applying the dye mixture.

8 Turn the block over and place it carefully on the stretched silk as centrally as possible. Using a rolling pin (kept specially for the purpose) or a clean roller, apply even pressure all over the block, so that the dye is transferred onto the silk. Take a little time to do this because it must be done thoroughly.

9 Carefully peel off the lino-cut, starting in one corner and taking care not to jog it and smudge the print.

10 The finished print will be quite uneven when this method is used, but remember it is being used as a means of drawing and laying down a composition rather than as a linocut in its own right. If the background is too solid you will not be able to work into it. Leave the print to dry thoroughly, then steam to fix (see page 48). Rinse in cold water, wash in warm soapy water (thoroughly, to remove all traces of thickener); rinse, dry, and iron on the wrong side. Do not be alarmed if a lot of black dye appears to wash out; this does happen with dark colours.

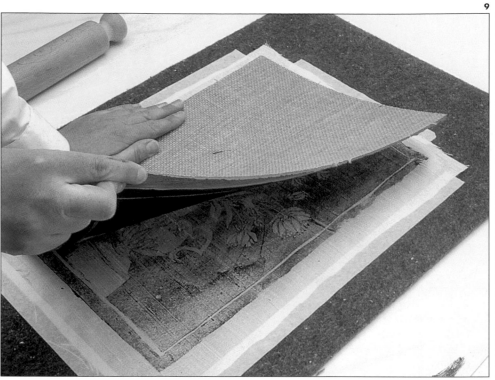

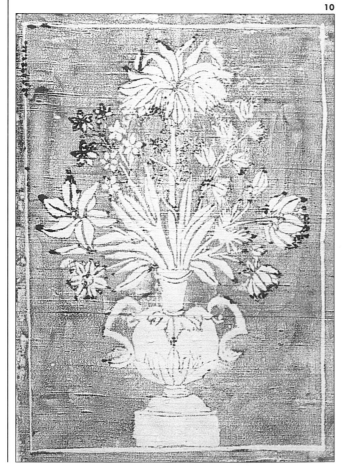

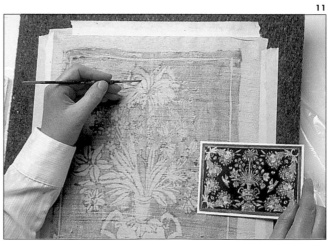

11 Using a soft no.2 brush and tiny amounts of colour – almost dry, in fact – and working from the original reference postcard, colour in the flowers and stems. Ready-to-use pigment (Javana Silk Paint) is used here.

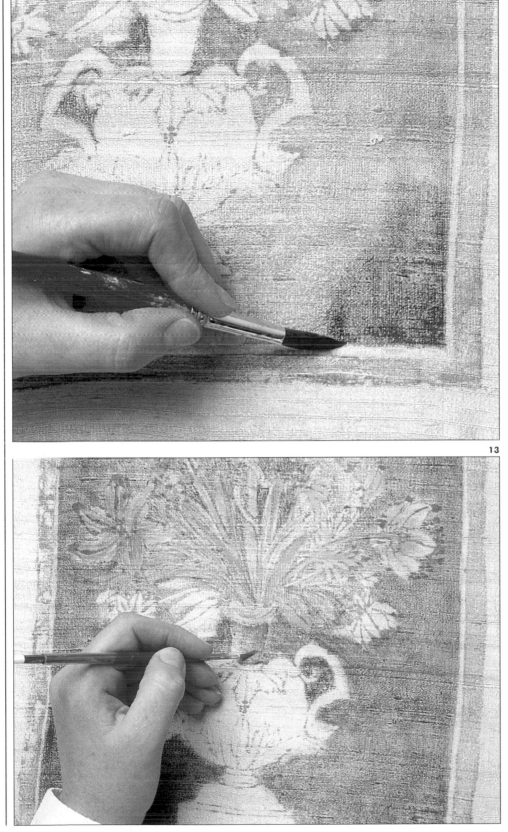

12 Use a larger (no.12) brush to shade in areas of the black background with Javana Silk Paint 8197 (very dark black), but only a very small amount should be applied at a time and spread gently with a fairly dry brush. Then use the smaller no.2 brush with black to get right into the edges of the coloured flowers and the area round the vase, giving depth to the background and making the details stand out more vividly against the black.

13 Use a soft no.6 brush to apply shading on the vase, where a little more colour can be built up in layers for the darker areas.

14

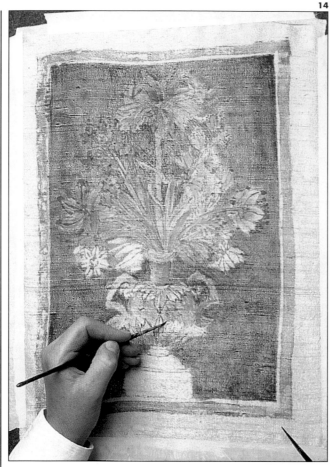

14 Then I returned to the small no.2 brush for filling in the detail on the vase.

15 Finally, paint the border in yellow with a no.2 brush and paint over the outer border in olive green mixed with Lapis Blue (8195), Maize Yellow (8192) and Cherry Red (8194).

16 Linocuts can make very bold images in themselves, largely because the nature of the cutting creates such a strong image. This project has used the medium in a highly controlled and formal way, making a 'negative' print. In other words, the background has been left uncut in order to receive the dye mixture and print a background which will give depth to any overpainting, while the detail has been cut out so that it can be coloured in afterwards.

You can, of course, develop the idea further, making linocuts which are 'positive': i.e. where the detail of the drawing is left raised to receive the dye mixture and the background is cut away. You can also experiment with different cut marks to give more vigour to your drawing. When cutting away backgrounds little bits of the lino inevitably get missed between the cuts and can add their own distinctive character to the piece .

To obtain a more solid, clearer print, try laying the silk directly – taking great care – on top of the inked block and press evenly before peeling off. For positive printing you can use pigment and binder or ready-to-use pigment mixed with thickener. Remember that the printed image will be the reverse of what you have drawn on the block.

15

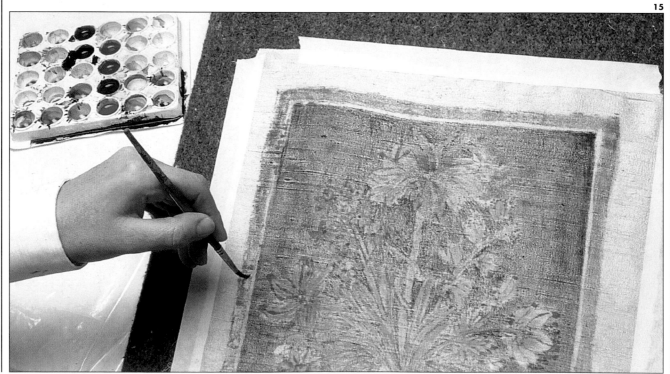

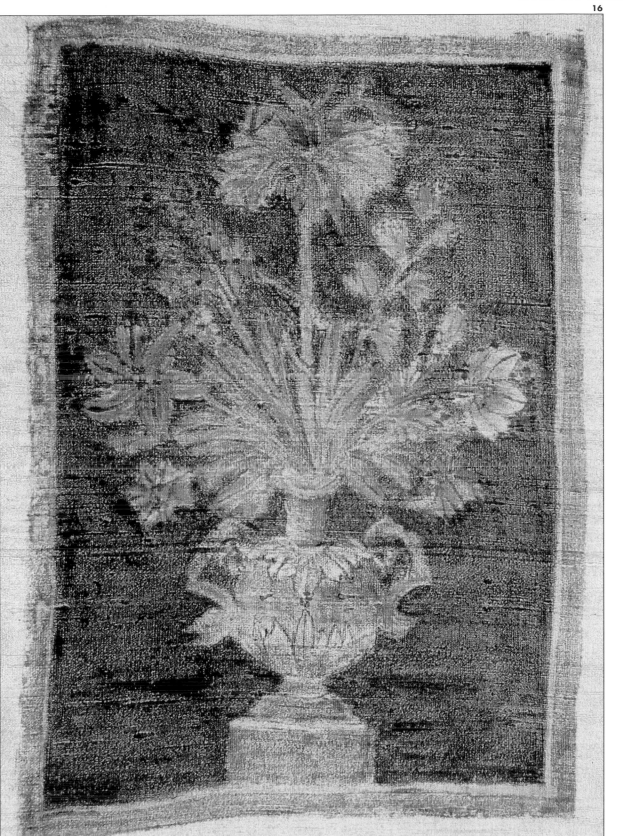

Fleur-de-Lys

LINOCUTS AND STENCILS

This project was inspired by a Florentine design of gold *fleur-de-lys* – the emblem of the city – on walls painted an intense blue which had then faded over the centuries. This project shows you how to paint a big, coloured background as well as how to cut a simple, symmetric stencil which can then be repeated on the silk. It is difficult to paint a background so that the colour is completely even with no streaks. Generally it is best to aim for results which are enhanced by the irregularities of the coloured background, which is frequently more lively and has more depth than a perfectly even ground. If you do want perfectly even coloured backgrounds, then silk is, of course, available in a range of beautiful commercially dyed colours which can be an inspiration in themselves.

If you are prepared to paint your own backgrounds, however, you can choose exactly which colours to use, mixing them wet on wet as you proceed. You might choose to use a particular colour mix that you have discovered while doing the stained glass project and work it up on a larger scale, building up tone and variation of colour.

For this project two shades of blue were used to imitate the faded nature of the walls in the reference picture. Specially designed stencil creme was used for the gold effect. This has a crumbly texture, ideal for stippling through the stencil. It is available in a wide range of colours, including metallics.

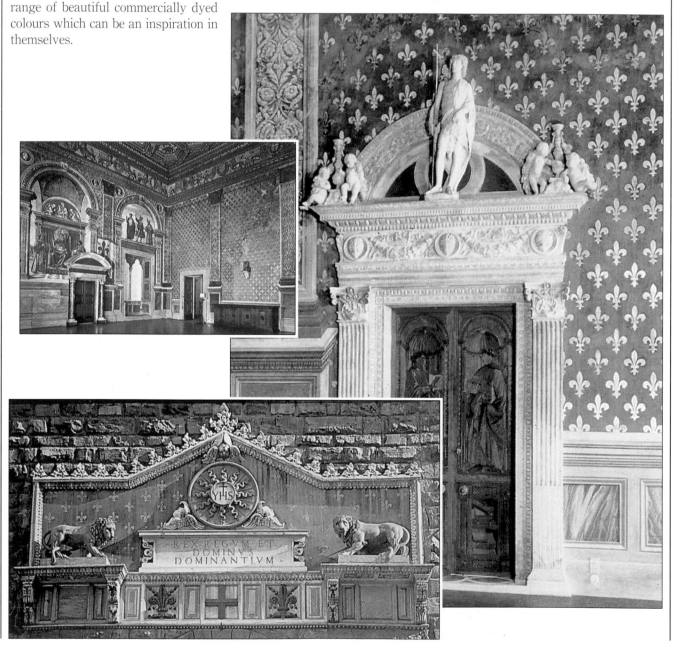

1 Before starting, you should make sure that the floor and wall against which you will be working is protected with plastic sheeting (see step 4).

Stretch approximately 5 ft. (1.5m) of taffeta on a large frame (see page 30). Fill an enamel dish with water and pour some Dupont Canard (2009) into another. Wearing rubber gloves and an apron or overalls apply the weakest solution of dye to the silk, dipping a 4 in. (10cm) bristle decorators' brush alternately into the water and a tiny amount of dye. Use strong, rhythmic brush strokes from top to bottom of the silk and then back up to the top. Repeat this until the whole silk is flooded with a wash of pale colour. It is important to keep painting while the silk is wet. Don't leave it to dry when you are halfway across, because you will get a pronounced streak where the dye has dried (unless, of course, that is the effect you want).

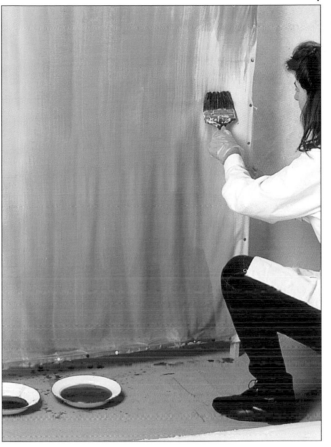

2 While the dye is still wet from the first step, pour some Dupont Cote D'Azur (2010) into another enamel dish and repeat step 1 using this darker blue with the turquoise and the water used in step 1.

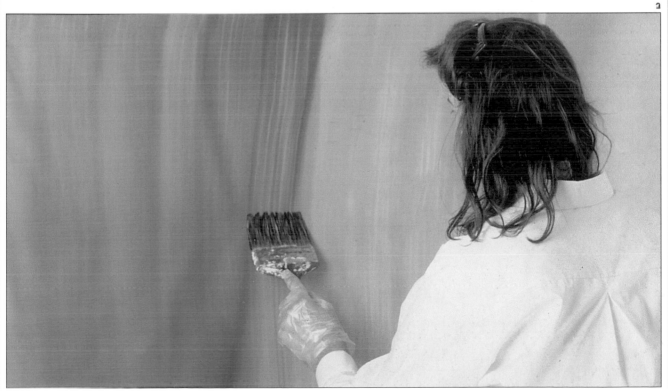

3

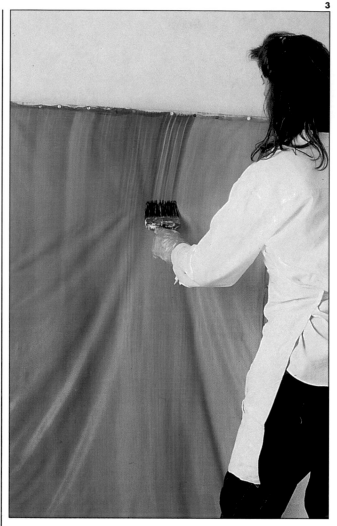

4

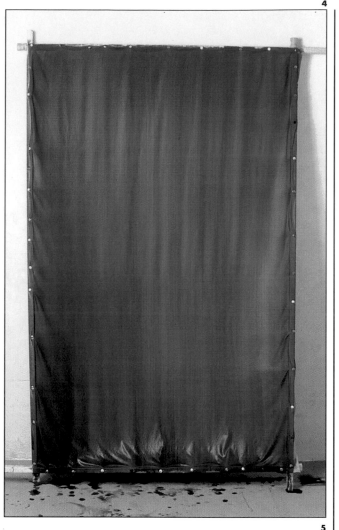

5

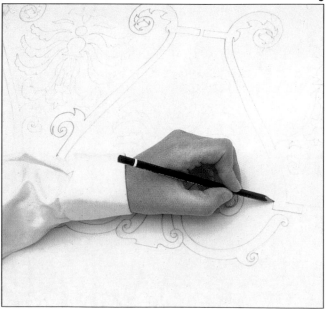

3 Repeat the layers, building up the proportion of dye to water as you go. Because of the stiff bristles on the decorators' brush you can build streaks of darker colour into the background as you go if you wish. The final effect is up to you.

4 The finished background will have a wonderful depth and intensity of colour. Note how much mess there is on the floor now. The plastic sheeting mentioned at the beginning really is necessary. The wall behind will get traces of dye on it, too, and so will you, so it is most important that you wear gloves and protective clothing. Leave the silk to dry; steam (see page 48); rinse in cold water; wash in warm soapy water, then rinse again, dry and iron on the wrong side.

5 Now you can prepare the stencils. The scroll border is a simple interpretation of the vertical pattern by the doorway in the reference picture. It is drawn up in pencil on paper and traced on to stencil paper. Do not cut it until you have cut out the simpler *fleur-de-lys* shapes and become more practised with using the craft knife.

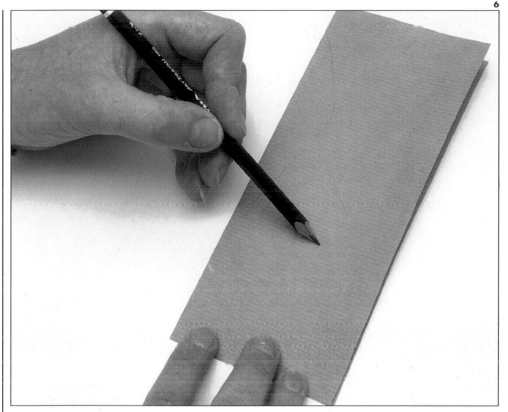

6 To cut the symmetrical *fleur-de-lys,* fold a piece of paper measuring 8x7 in. (20.5x18cm) lengthways down the centre. Using a pencil, sketch in one half of the *fleur-de-lys.*

7 The fold acts as the axis of symmetry so you only have to draw one half of the *fleur-de-lys.*

8 Re-fold the paper and cut around the shape of the half *fleur-de-lys* you have drawn. The finished *fleur-de-lys* should be about 6½ in. (16.5cm) in height.

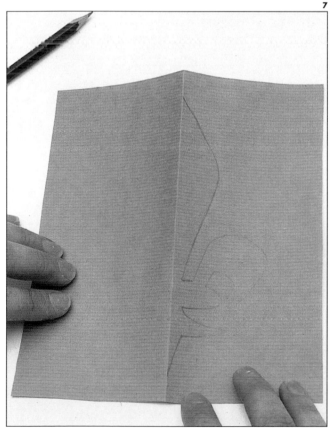

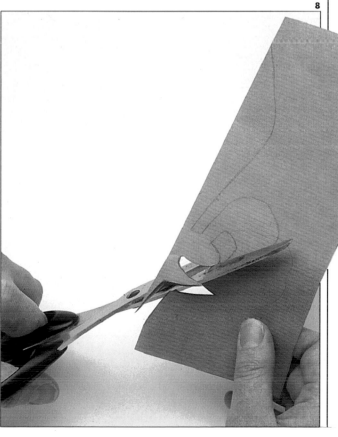

9 On tracing paper draw a grid of rectangles, each measuring 6x6½ in. (15x16.5cm). On one row of the grid – horizontally – trace around the *fleur-de-lys* four times in four separate rectangles, each time positioning the *fleur-de-lys* in the centre of the rectangle. Repeat the process three times on the row below. This time place the centre of the *fleur-de-lys* on a vertical line so that the designs on the new line are positioned between those on the line above.

10 Trace the repeated pattern of *fleur-de-lys* on to stencil paper or strong brown wrapping paper. Place the stencil paper on a cutting board and cut around the *fleur-de-lys* shapes with a craft knife.

Always keep the hand not holding the knife **in front** of the hand which is cutting and always cut away from that hand and your body. Retractable craft knives are available which are much safer to use and highly recommended.

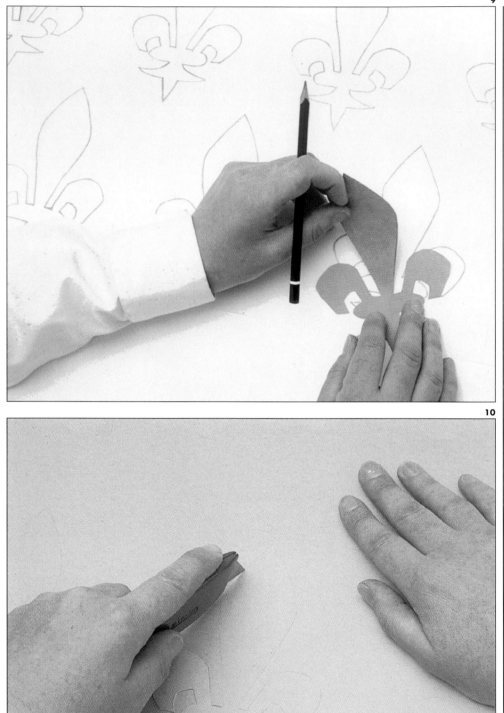

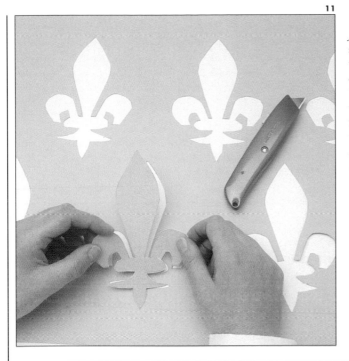

11 As you cut around each *fleur-de-lys,* lift it out of the stencil paper. Be careful that you have cut right through all of the stencil paper before you lift the design out, to avoid tearing. When you have finished cutting the *fleur-de-lys* you should feel more confident about cutting the more complicated scroll border on a separate piece of paper.

12 Place a piece of underfelt or an old blanket on a flat surface – table or large board – and tape it into place with masking tape. Secure the silk background – now fixed, washed and ironed – to the underblanket with double-sided adhesive tape.

Lay the stencil border on the silk in a central position approximately 6 in. (15cm) from the bottom of the silk. Secure it at the corners with masking tape. Using a medium-sized stippling brush, apply gold stencil creme using the brush upright and making short, sharp downward dabs onto the silk (stippling). You can vary the depth of shade by applying differing layers of the creme as you go.

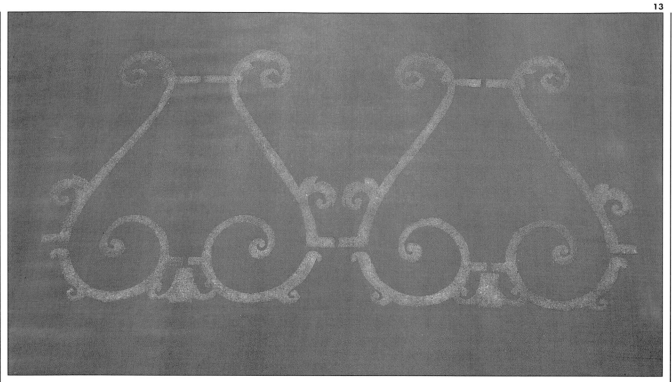

13 Check that you have filled in the whole stencil shape before you move on to the next one and then check again when you have finished. Carefully remove the stencil paper, lifting straight up by the edges to avoid smudges. The stencil creme takes up to 24 hours before it is completely dry, but it is possible to continue building up the stencils immediately, as long as you are very careful not to pull the stencil paper across the newly painted surface and smudge it.

14 Position the *fleur-de-lys* stencil carefully above the scroll pattern and lower it gently on to the cloth, taking care of the scroll border. Secure the corners of the stencil paper with masking tape and proceed as at step 12. Repeat as necessary. The bottom part of the scroll of the border can be used on its own as vertical and top borders and the large scrolls can each be filled in with a *fleur-de-lys*.

15 Once you have got used to positioning the stencils accurately, and become confident about working over and around the parts that are still wet, then this becomes a very simple and direct method to use. Coupled with the hand-painted backgrounds, stencils can create very dramatic effects. They can be used for formal repeated patterns or positioned randomly for a more spontaneous effect. Individual parts of the stencils can also be used.

Specially formulated stencil creme is perfect for the beginner, as its crumbly texture makes it ideal for the stippling technique used to lay the colour down. As you become more proficient you may like to experiment with thickened pigments or thickened dyes (remember to fix them appropriately). They are more difficult to use, being stickier, but can still be very effective.

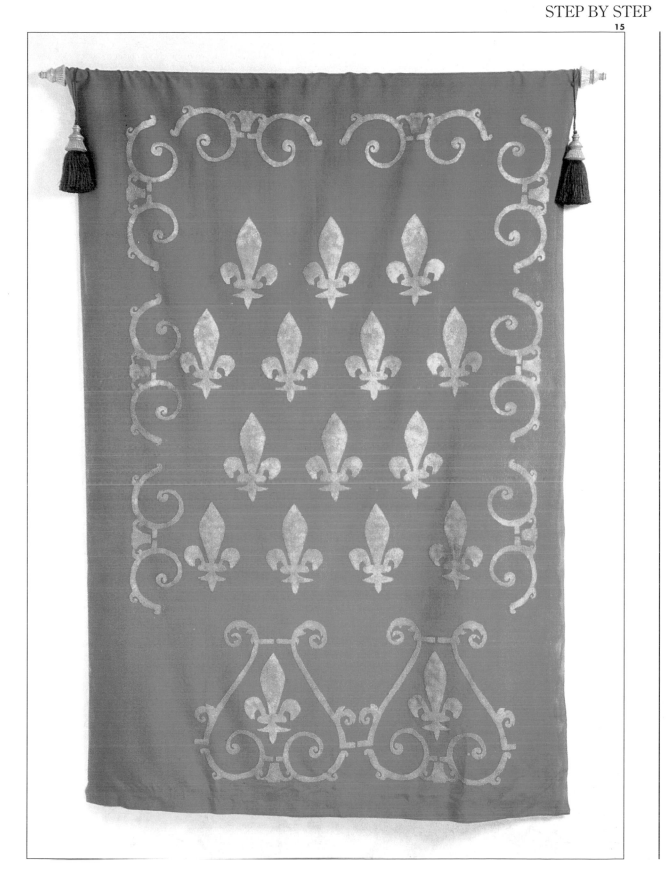

Chapter 6
Decorative Panels

The two projects in this chapter are derived from decorative traditions of painting known as 'grotesque'. One is based on a wall painting found at Boscotrecase, near Pompeii, dating from around 11-15B.C. The other is a panel based on Renaissance decorative motifs in the Palazzo Farnese di Caprarola and the Palazzo Vecchio which were inspired by the discovery of early wall paintings of the kind found in Boscotrecase. (The term 'grotesque' derives from the grottoes in which these paintings were found.)

In both projects opaque white pigment is used both on its own and as a base for mixing colours to achieve a chalky effect quite different from dyes or ordinary pigment and binder.

The Italian 'Renaissance' grotesque panel is used to demonstrate how the opaque white can complement the natural colour of unbleached silk.

The black 'Pompeian' panel shows how the opaque white will sit on the surface of the densest of coloured backgrounds (dye would be absorbed by the black background, white pigment and binder or ready-to-use pigment sink without much trace on black).

A very limited, understated palette has been used in both pieces, but the results are quite different. While bright vibrant colours obtainable on silk can be very exciting these two projects show the more subtle, understated effects which can be achieved.

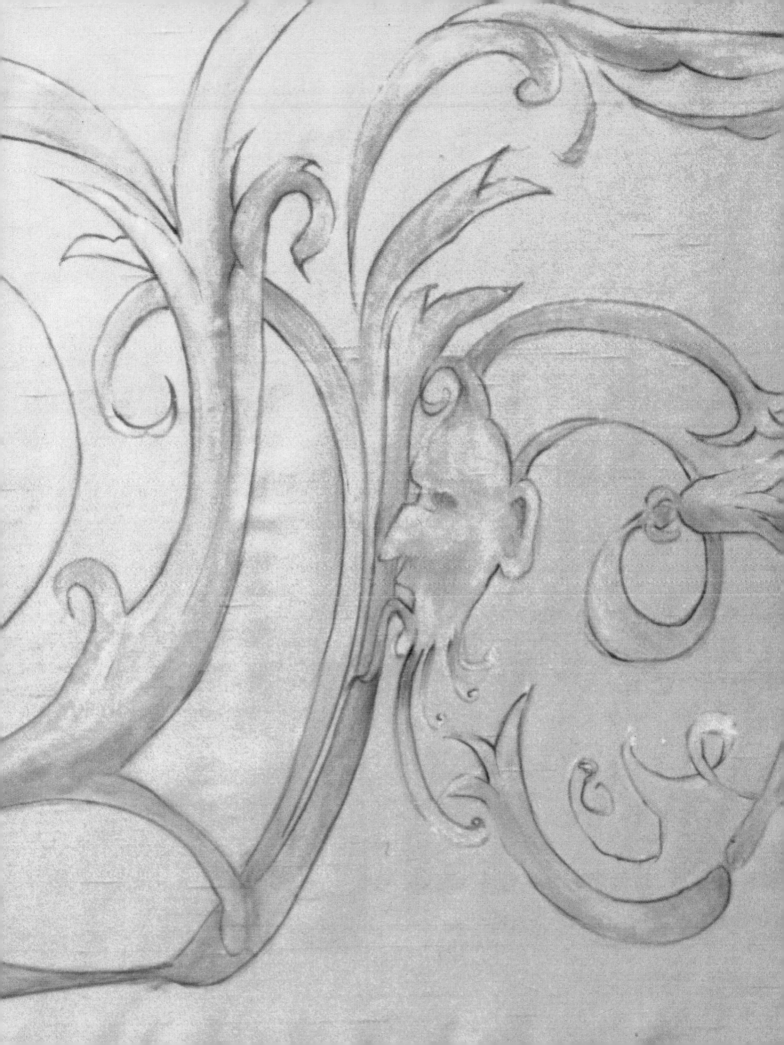

Italian Grotesque

DECORATIVE PANELS

The Renaissance 'grotesque' decoration which inspired this project was first influenced by contemporary discoveries of wall-paintings of the kind reflected in the other project in this chapter. While strong colour was often used in such paintings, centuries of exposure to the air and general wear-and-tear have caused their brilliance to fade.

This seemed, therefore, a good subject to use in conjunction with an unpainted silk background. An unbleached tussah silk was chosen for the project; this has a small, irregular slub and a beautiful pale, creamy colour.

All the media in the project, including the felt-tip pens, use pigment, making all the stages easy to fix.

Felt-tip pens which have been designed specifically for use on textiles are quite revolutionary. You can now draw exactly on cloth with a medium which can be fixed simply by ironing. The fine, flowing, easy-to-control lines or cross-hatched marks which can be drawn in this way expand the range of techniques available to the painter on silk. In this project they are used as a base for the whole composition and then worked over with pigment to camouflage their excessively graphic nature, which is unsuitable here but could be perfect for expressing other ideas.

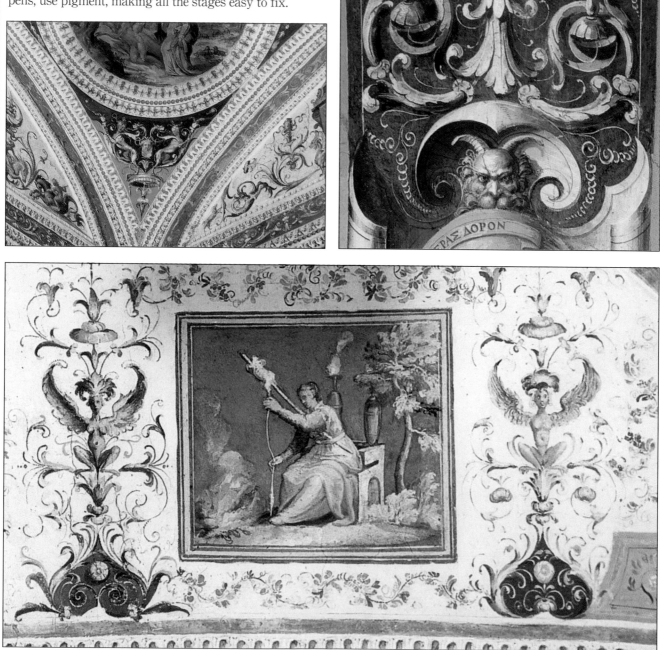

1 Working from the original reference a very loose, simple sketch was made roughly on paper, using different elements from a number of wall-paintings to produce a long rectangular composition. You can use this sketch as the basis for your project, working from it freehand, or follow the illustration in step 6.

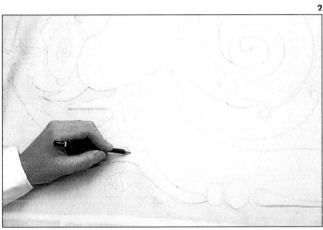

2 If you are a confident draughtsman it is possible to work using a 2B pencil directly from the sketch on to the silk. This should measure approximately 48x24 in. (122x60cm) and be stretched on to a padded board (see page 32) measuring no less than 52x28 in. (132x71cm). Draw lightly, so that any mistakes can be rubbed off the silk, using a pencil eraser if necessary. Do not worry if you cannot erase mistakes entirely; they are, after all, a part of the drawing process.

If you feel daunted by the prospect of drawing straight on to this beautiful large piece of clean silk, then work the design out on a sheet of paper the same size as the silk (stick several sheets together or use paper off a roll) and trace out the whole composition in pencil. Cut around the outside of the main, large scroll shapes but do not separate them. Tape the tracing to the silk with small pieces of masking tape, then lightly draw around the edge of the main cut shapes on the silk, using a 2B pencil.

3 When you have drawn around the main shapes start to cut into the tracing so that you can reach the inner scroll shapes. If you try to cut all the tracing out at once, it will become impossible to handle. Concentrate on small areas at a time, tracing around the shapes one by one as you cut them.

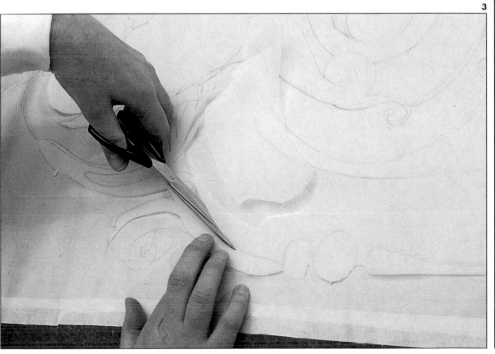

4 Once the main parts of the composition are in place, it becomes much easier to put in the details freehand.

5 Using a Javana art marker for fabrics (Brown 90608), go over the whole composition, making swift, light marks. You can practise with an ordinary felt-tip pen on paper first if you are not very confident.

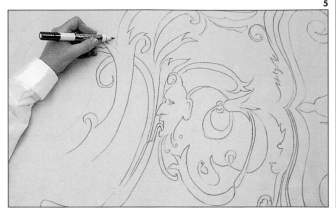

6 This is the final composition if you wish to use it as a guide.

7 Take a white wax crayon specially made for textile use and, using its flat side, work across the whole composition, applying a light coat of wax inside the outlines to the scroll shapes, mask, etc.

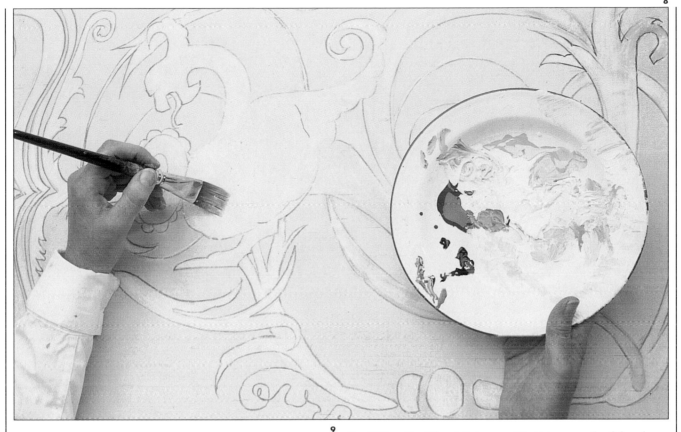

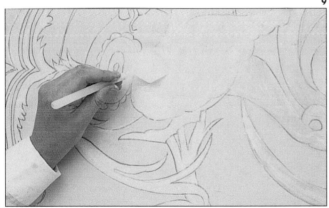

8 With a 1 in. (2.5 cm) flat, soft brush, lightly paint over the wax with Bricoprint Opaque White T.

9 If the white becomes too thick, it can be partly scraped off while still wet with a plastic glue spreader.

10 Using a small, soft no. 2 brush, lightly obscure some of the brown felt-tip outlines and details with opaque white.

11 Using a no. 6 soft brush, highlight the light parts of the composition with opaque white mixed with a tiny amount of Helizarin Yellow G and Red BT. Mix the colours into the white on an enamel dish, so that you can intermix them freely as you work. Shade the yellow off into the white in subtle gradations.

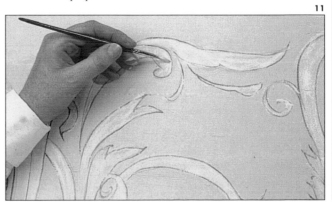

103

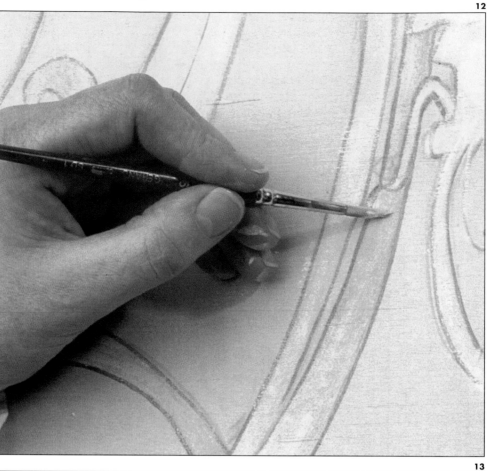

12 With a no. 6 soft brush, mix a tiny amount of Helizarin Brown RBT on the end of your brush with some of the white from the enamel dish. Use this with a fraction of Helizarin Black TT mixed on the dish with white for shading those areas of the composition which, when darkened will emphasize the shape of the scrolls. If the white pigment and colours have a tendency to dry up quickly on the dish, spray them lightly with water from a plant spray. This may make them look a bit messy, but it does allow them to remain workable. If you have to leave the colours on the dish, cover it with clingfilm. Opaque white does dry very fast and it is advisable to use it in small quantities, mixing fresh amounts each time you need it.

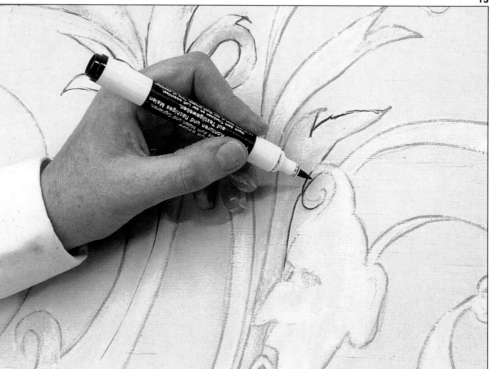

13 Using a Javana felt marker for fabric (Black 90618) work lightly over the outlines to give weight to the rhythm of the curved outlines.

14 If the black looks too heavy and obtrusive, mask it with a little opaque white applied with the no. 6 brush.

15 Now you should stand back from the panel and have a good look at it. Does the use of highlighting and shading emphasize the scrolling patterns or not? Keep working on the highlighting and shading until the piece has a swirling flow which undulates along its whole length.

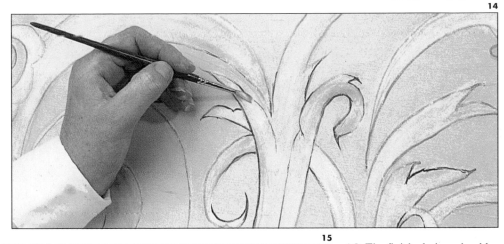

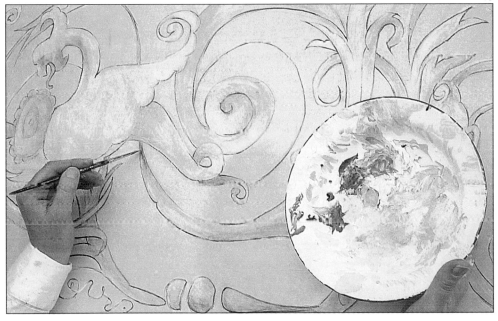

16 The finished piece should be balanced and rhythmic. The shading and highlighting must give emphasis to the curve of the lines of the composition. The overall effect should be light, providing a contrast between the painted areas and the natural, subdued beauty of the silk itself. This project should start you thinking about ways of using the natural tones of the silk as part of your work, rather than changing its essential nature by simply applying strong colour.

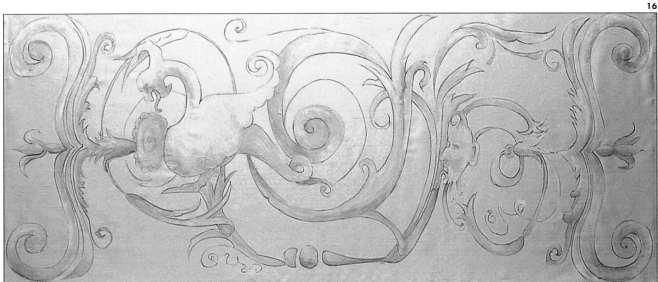

Black Pompeian Panel

DECORATIVE PANELS

This project was inspired by a visit to the Metropolitan Museum of Art in New York which has an extensive collection of 'fragments' – in reality these are quite large – of wall paintings from excavations at Boscoreale and Boscotrecase, near Pompeii. As fragments, some of the pieces have the quality of abstract paintings, composed of areas of worn but intense colour. Many also incorporate architectural detail as well as images drawn from the natural world.

Apart from the applied decoration, one of the most striking aspects of these paintings is the texture of the wall surface and the depth of colour still surviving, even in the ones with very dark backgrounds.

Silk noile was chosen for this project. This is one of the most fluid of the matte silks, with a graceful quality which allows it to be draped easily. It also has a distinctive surface texture, with flecks and a slight roughness not unlike some kinds of stone. It seemed the ideal surface for the project, in which the black background is built up layer upon layer to give depth, while the surface breaks up the brush strokes with which the opaque white pigment is applied, giving it a 'distressed' look.

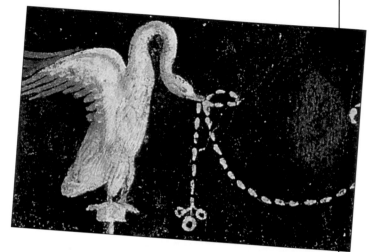

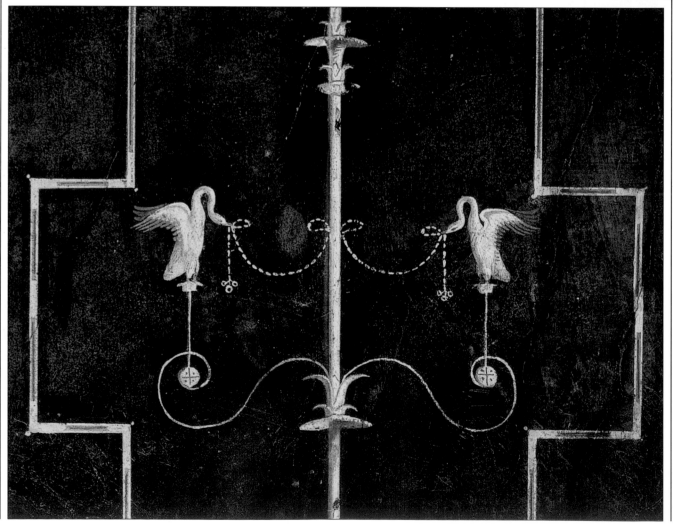

1

2

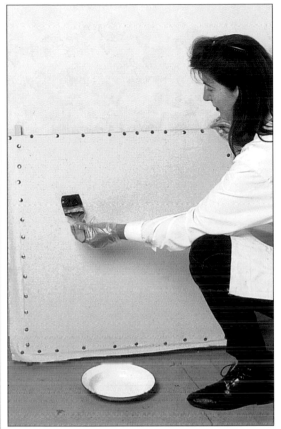

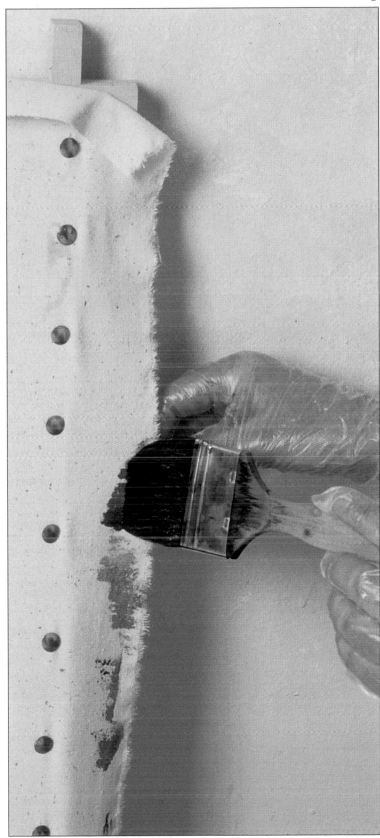

1 Stretch a square of silk noile measuring approximately 36x36 in. (91.5x91.5cm) on to a small frame (see page 30). First make sure that you are wearing rubber gloves then, using a 2½ in. (6cm) flat, soft brush, roughly paint the silk with clear gutta. Just paint here and there in broad strokes, but not all over the surface. This will resist the colour which will be painted over it and help to add to the worn, layered effect of the background. Then leave the gutta to dry.

2 Ready-to-use pigment (Javana Silk Paint) is used here. Turquoise (8113), Bordeaux (8117) and Sun Yellow (8122) are mixed together to make a bluish, greenish grey. Mix in an enamel dish. Test the colour on a spare piece of silk until it looks similar to the one in the illustration here.

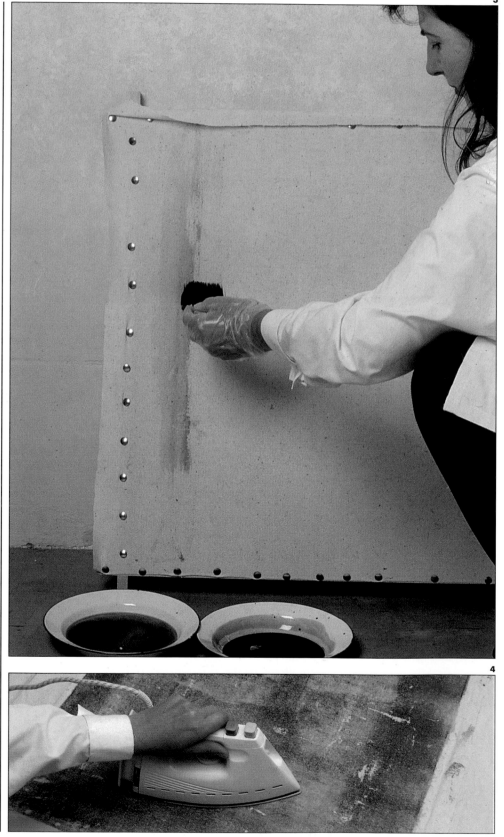

3

3 Using water from a second enamel dish, cover the silk with quick brush strokes with the soft, flat 2½ in. (6cm) brush, literally slapping the mixture on from side to side and up and down until the whole area is covered, dipping the brush alternately into the colour and the water as you paint. Keep building up the layers until the colour looks quite dark but also quite roughly textured. Leave it to dry thoroughly.

4

4 When the piece is completely dry, remove it from the frame and iron for three minutes on the wrong side on the cotton setting. Wash in warm soapy water, rinse, dry, and iron on the wrong side.

5 Re-stretch the silk on the frame. Either use black lining paint or mix Helizarin Black TT with Bricoprint Binder SF20 to make a dense black. Paint roughly in big strokes all over the silk, using the 2½ in. (6cm) brush, dipping it into the water as you work, until the surface is covered. Leave to dry thoroughly. The black should now look quite dark.

6 When the silk is completely dry, fix the pigment by ironing for three minutes on the wrong side on the cotton setting. Wash in warm soapy water; rinse, dry, iron on the wrong side, and re-stretch on the frame. The silk will now look considerably paler but you will see that a worn, textured background is beginning to appear.

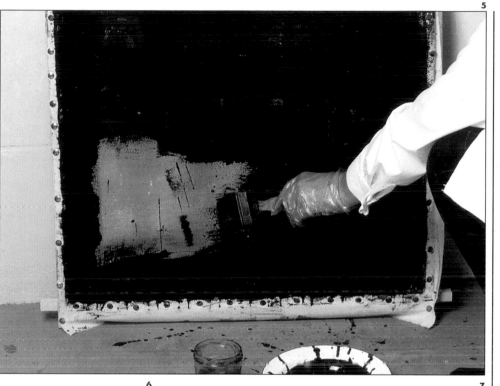

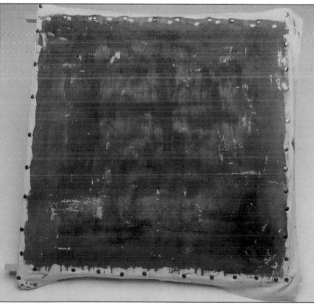

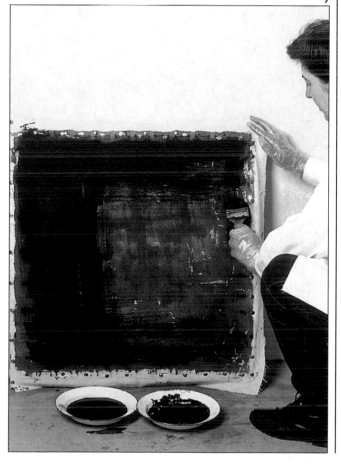

7 Repeat steps 5 and 6 once or twice more, until the surface – when fixed, washed and ironed – resembles an old blackboard.

8 Transfer the silk to a padded board (see page 32) measuring no less than 40x 40 in. (102x102cm). Secure it with masking tape. Measure the centre of the silk and, using tailor's chalk and a ruler, draw a vertical line from head to foot through the centre.

At the top measure 9½ in. (24cm) to the right of the centre line and draw a vertical line 13½ in. (34.5cm) long parallel with the centre line. Interrupt drawing the line but leave the ruler on the silk. Measure a further 11½ in. (29cm) down and resume the line from this point, continuing down to the foot of the silk. Where the line is broken measure 3 in. (7.5cm) to the right at each of the two points and draw a 3 in. (7.5cm) horizontal line. Join these two horizontal lines together with a vertical line, 11½ in. (29cm) long. (The illustration here shows the right-hand side of the composition.) The process needs to be repeated

symmetrically on the left-hand side of the composition, using the central line as the axis of symmetry. If this seems too strictly mathematical, do it by eye and copy on the other side. Then place the ruler vertically on top of the centre line and rule down either side of it with the chalk to make a 1in. (2.5cm) wide stripe running through the silk from head to foot.

9 Using a soft no.6 brush and Bricoprint Opaque White T or other opaque white textile medium, roughly start to fill in the central pole, using the white quite thickly and adding water when necessary on the brush to make the white go on more easily. Use light, quick brush strokes, so that some of the black background shows through. While the white is still wet, mix a little brown into it. Javana Silk Paint is used here, colour Brown (8107), to fill in shading and details of leaves, etc. on the wet white.

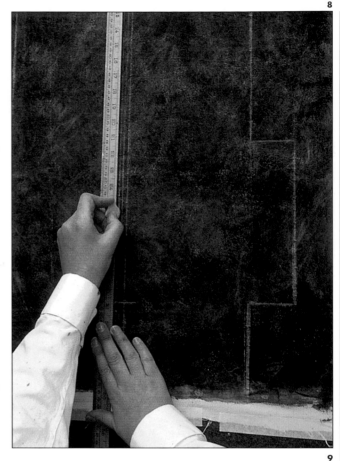

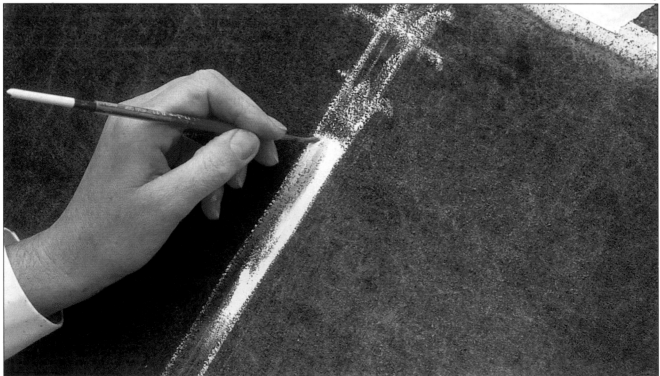

10 When the central pole is finished, move on to the vertical lines at the sides and start to fill in using the same methods with a small, soft 00 brush and opaque white and brown. The white is laid down over the chalk line to a width of approximately ⅜in. (1cm), using long straight brush strokes to make two vertical lines ⅜in. (1cm) apart which are then filled in. Use the brush against a ruler if you want really straight lines. The edges of the central pole can be made neater in the same way. Stop the white paint here and there on the vertical lines using a straight brush stroke.

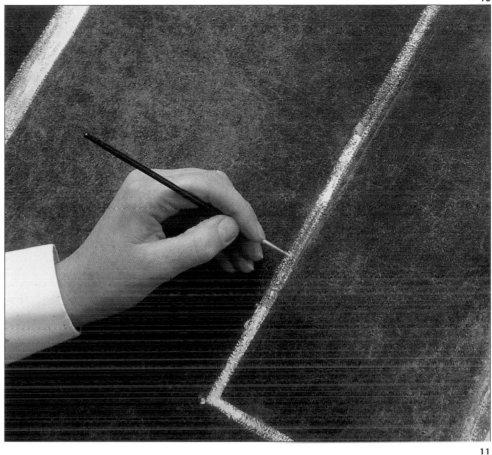

11 In the gaps in the white lines lay down a little brown, finishing off with a straight line and blending a little into the white in places.

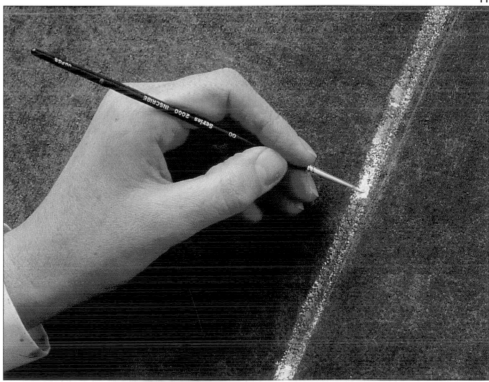

12 In the centre of the space between the central pole and the vertical side lines paint a straight vertical line in white with the 00 brush and a ruler. This should measure 4 in. (10cm). Repeat symmetrically on the other side. Draw the curved line on one side with tailor's chalk to join the central pole to a circle at the base of the 4 in. (10cm) vertical line and paint in with white blended with a tiny bit of brown. Working on one side only, rough in the outline of the bird with tailor's chalk and paint with the 00 brush. See step 15. Leave to dry.

13 Now trace the bird and the curved lines which join it to the central pole. Then cut around the outside of the tracing of the bird's wings and around the curved lines. Do not cut out the bird's chest at this point.

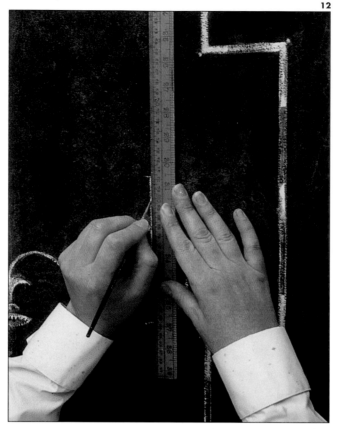

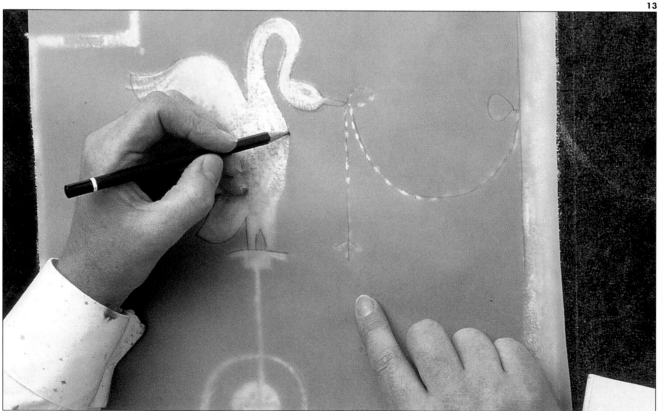

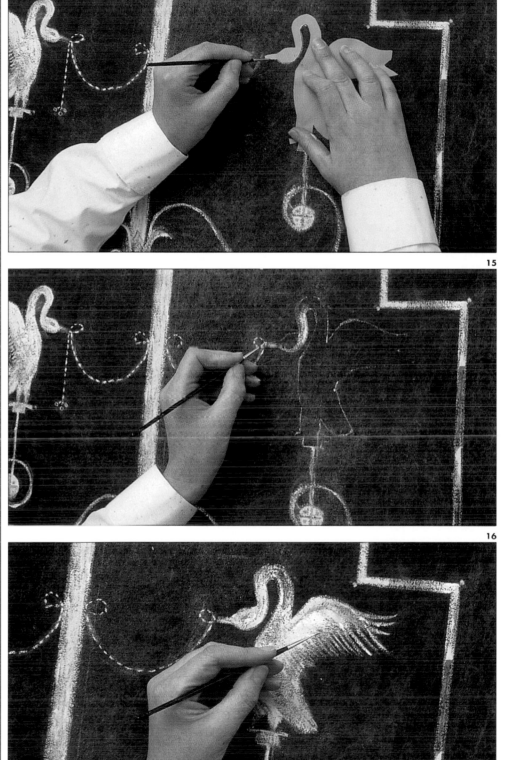

14 Position the tracing on the other side of the pole. Trace around the cut-out shape of the curved lines using the 00 brush and opaque white to make very light marks. When you have traced the curved lines and the wings of the bird, cut out the rest of the bird, line it up with the previous tracing painted on the silk and trace round the edge, lightly using the 00 brush and opaque white.

15 Paint in the bird, starting first with opaque white applied roughly. This allows the background to show through and act as shading.

16 Further shading and detail (eyes, beak, wing feathers and legs) can be added wet on wet with the brown, but keep your brush strokes light and do not overload the brush, so that the black background is not obscured and can still act as shading.

17 Using a black wax crayon specially intended for textile use, shade into the background using the flat side to deepen the black around the detail, making it stand out more.

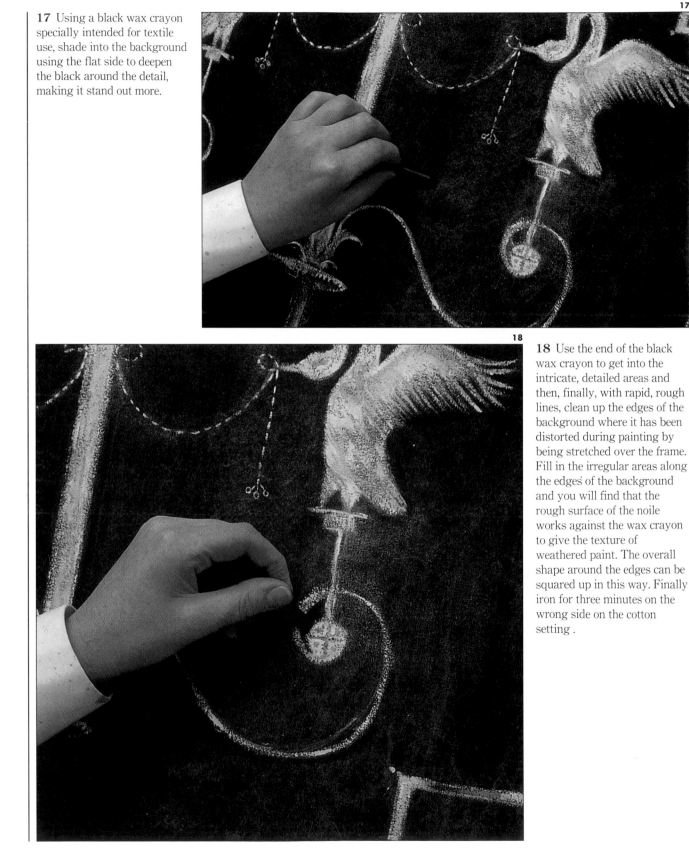

18

18 Use the end of the black wax crayon to get into the intricate, detailed areas and then, finally, with rapid, rough lines, clean up the edges of the background where it has been distorted during painting by being stretched over the frame. Fill in the irregular areas along the edges of the background and you will find that the rough surface of the noile works against the wax crayon to give the texture of weathered paint. The overall shape around the edges can be squared up in this way. Finally iron for three minutes on the wrong side on the cotton setting .

19 This project shows the contrast between the free, broad-stroke way of building up the background with the big brush and the delicate overpainting of the detail. It may lead you to want to abandon small brushes and detail in favour of big, multi-layered textural pieces. Or you may wish to build on the skill you are developing in handling detail.

Alternatively you may see new possibilities in using painted grounds and detail together. Certainly the noile used here absorbs the colour and gives a very different effect from the taffeta used in the *'fleur-de-lys'* project. You should now be developing ideas of your own about how different types of silk work with colour and how you would use those differences in relation to the different media at your disposal.

19

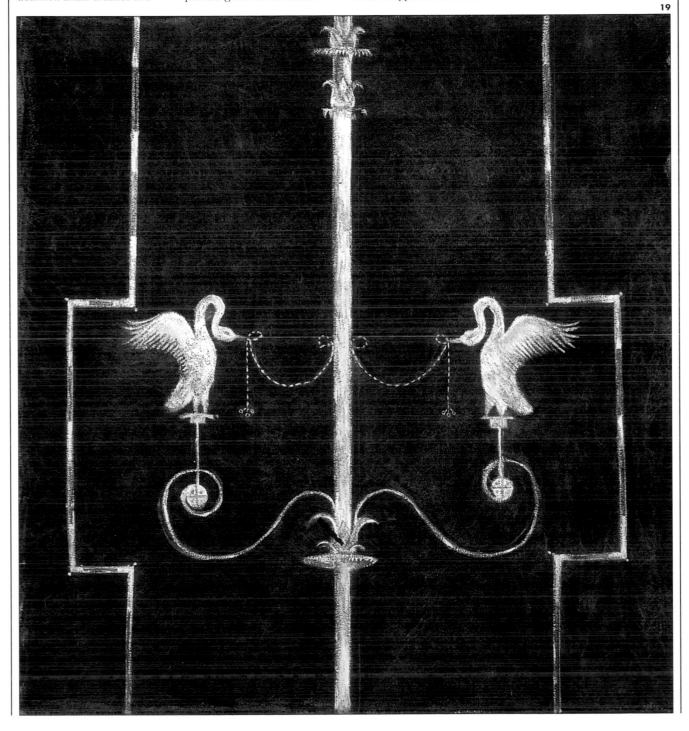

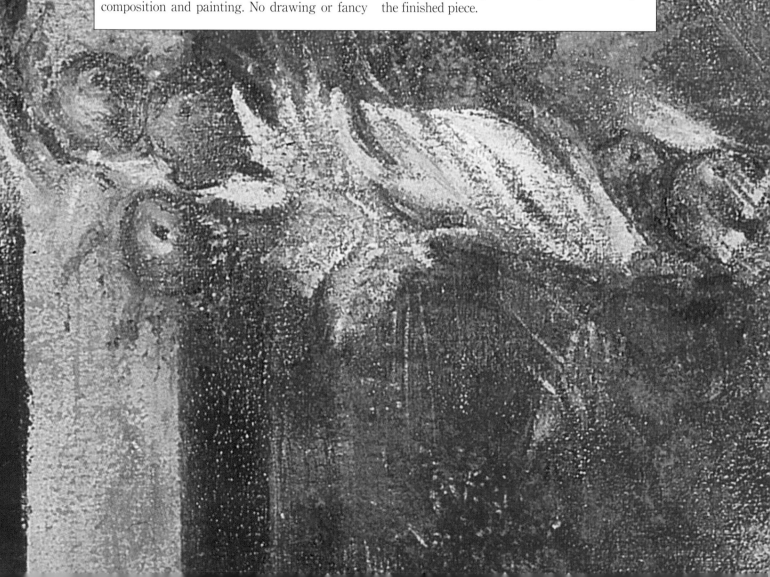

Chapter 7
Painterly Effects

The projects in the preceding three chapters have demonstrated the use of the three different textile media and the way they can be combined with the various surface qualities of silk to give a wide range of effects. These two final projects develop the experience you have gained so far. You can now explore ways of using the unique surface quality of silk with the appropriate media to produce pieces which take full advantage of the material as a ground for painting.

The icon project uses extremely simple methods and is quite suitable for a beginner. It is also a good project to try if you have found some of the other projects rather complex in terms of composition and painting. No drawing or fancy brushwork is necessary as we use a method of transferring photocopies directly on to fabric. Surprisingly sophisticated results can be achieved with minimum technical complications.

In the final project (based on another of the Pompeian fragments in the Metropolitan Museum of Art) more complicated techniques are used. Many of the methods already explored are brought together, with dye being used to create the intense, glowing background, while colour mixed with binder, as well as opaque white mixed with colour, are used for overpainting.

In both projects the character of the surface of the silk is an important aspect of the vitality of the finished piece.

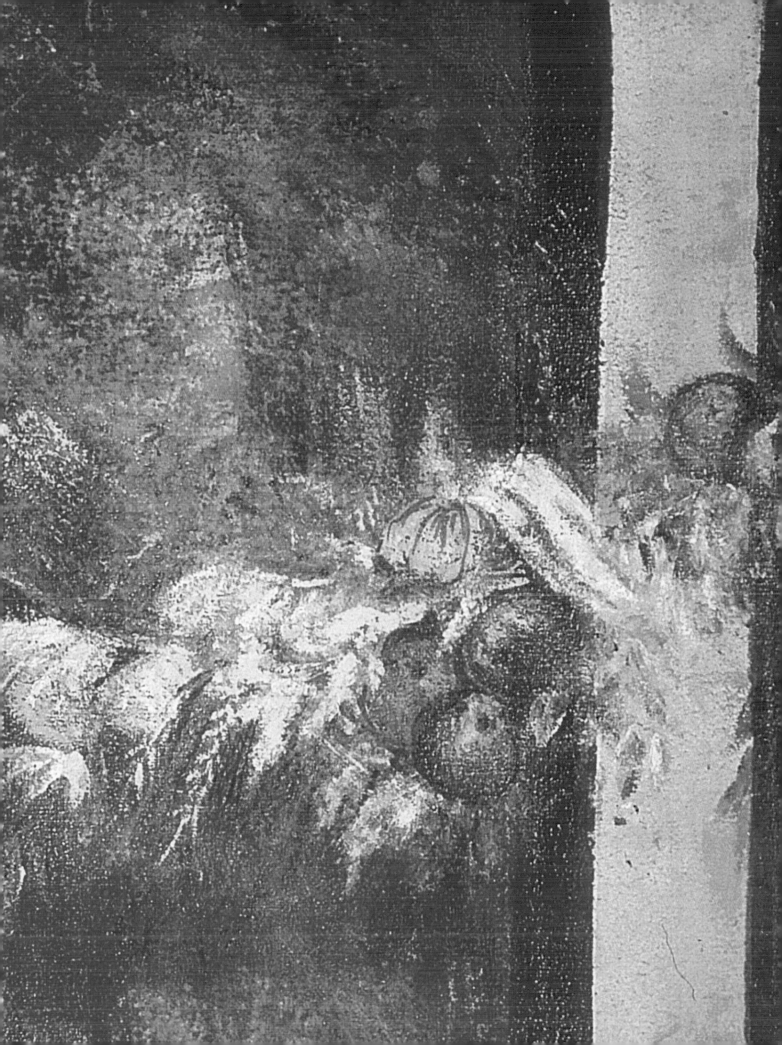

Icon

PAINTERLY EFFECTS

This project was inspired by icon paintings. Older examples of such paintings – richly embellished with gold and even sometimes with precious stones as an expression of veneration towards the religious subjects depicted – have often suffered considerable wear over the centuries. Many of the paintings now have a faded, textural quality. This aspect is given special emphasis in this project.

Using manufacturers' instructions, flawless copies of photocopied images can be transferred directly on to fabric, but in this project the process was modified to produce a partly destroyed image to resemble an older icon. The photocopies can be made in full colour (it is possible to change the colours during the photocopy process) or black and white as in this project, where the image was tinted with ready-to-use pigment.

Remember when you choose an image that you should not infringe copyright laws. You can, if you wish, have your own photographs, drawings or paintings photocopied for use with this technique. When the image used here was photocopied, the colours came out darker than in the original. Remember that the transfer process will result in the image on the cloth being the opposite way round to the original photocopy. If you want the image to be the same way round (e.g. if it has lettering on it) then make sure you have the image reversed. This can either be done as part of the process during photocopying on some colour copiers (which can also print in black and white if required) or you can take a copy on to acetate, reverse it, and take a reverse copy on paper for use with the transfer method. Most photocopy shops with these facilities are very helpful about experimenting with your artwork.

A herring-bone silk was chosen for the piece. It has a slubby surface and subtle streaks of golden colour which, combined with the pattern of the weave, all interact with the stained background and help to set off the metallic pigments. It also contrasts well with the transferred image, which stays on the surface of the cloth and reveals the silk where it is pulled away.

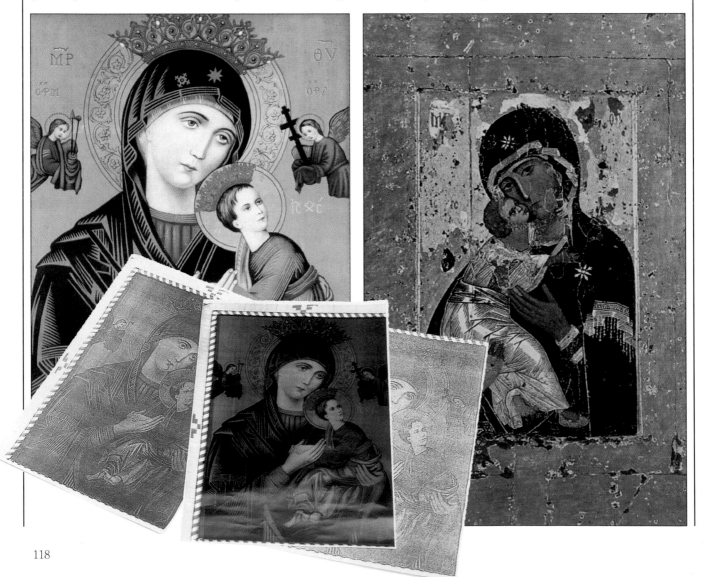

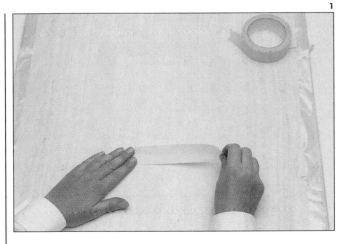

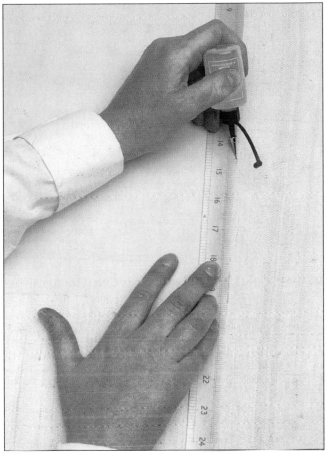

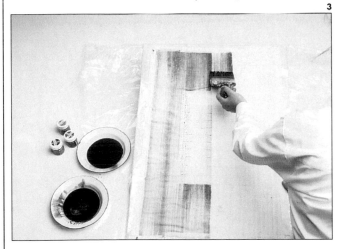

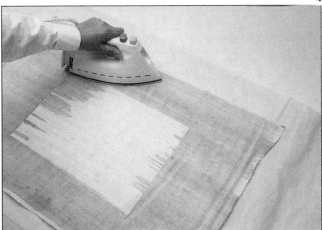

1 Stretch a piece of herring-bone silk 30x20 in. (76x51cm) on to a previously padded board (see page 32) measuring not less than 34x24 in. (86.5x61cm). Using 2 in. (5cm) masking tape, mask off the centre of the silk in a rectangle measuring 15x10½ in (38x26.5cm). You should start 7½ in. (19cm) from the top of the silk.

2 Using clear gutta in a plastic container with a nozzle (see page 45) draw around the outside of the masked rectangle using a ruler and the edge of the tape as a guide. This will, to some extent, resist the colour applied next and define the edge of the border. Although it will not prevent all the colour from seeping under the tape, as the herring-bone silk is quite thick, it will help to control the amount which seeps through.

3 Using ready-to-use pigment – Javana colour for silk, Brown (8107) with a little Cherry (8194) and Intense Sun Yellow (8122) mixed together in an enamel dish – and a 4 in. (10cm) decorators' bristle brush; first dip the brush into water and then pick up a small amount of the brown on it. Using smooth, straight brush strokes, paint straight down the silk and over the masking tape from top to bottom. Repeat from side to side, then leave to dry thoroughly. Remove the masking tape and discard.

4 Iron on the wrong side for three minutes, on the cotton setting, to fix. Rinse in cold water, wash in warm soapy water; rinse, dry and iron on the wrong side.

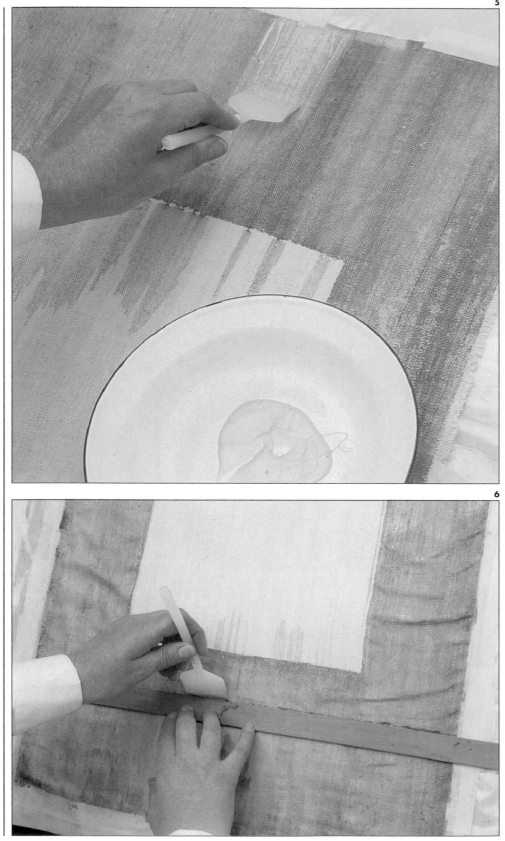

5 Re-stretch the silk on the board. Pour some gold ready-to-use pigment into an enamel dish – Javana lining paint, Light Gold (814750) – and apply to the silk, using a 2 in. (5cm) wide plastic glue spreader, following the vertical direction of the brown background. Be careful to stop at the edge of the border. It should not be necessary to mask the silk again, as it is quite easy to control the gold using this method.

6 Using brown metallic ready-to-use pigment – Javana lining paint Brown (813350) – wet on wet with the gold, and wet on dry, with the reference picture of the painting as a guide, start to work in the darker areas of the border, including the lines. These can be put in, using a ruler. Remember to wipe the ruler with a cloth in between making the lines to prevent smudging. You can use different shades of gold to build up intensity. Leave to dry.

7 Choose the photocopied image you are going to use. Don't forget that the transferred image on the silk will be the reverse of the original. Lay the photocopy, image side up, on a piece of plastic or silver foil. Paint Dylon Colorfun Image Maker on to the photocopied image, using a clean 1in. (2.5cm) flat, decorators' bristle brush. Vary the thickness of the Image Maker medium, taking care to paint a layer thick enough to obscure the image over the areas you want to transfer properly, and only a thin layer on those parts you want subsequently to peel away to achieve the worn effect on the finished piece (usually at the head, foot and edges). You may want to experiment with this step (and nos. 8-15) on a spare piece of calico before doing it on the silk to get some idea of how the medium works.

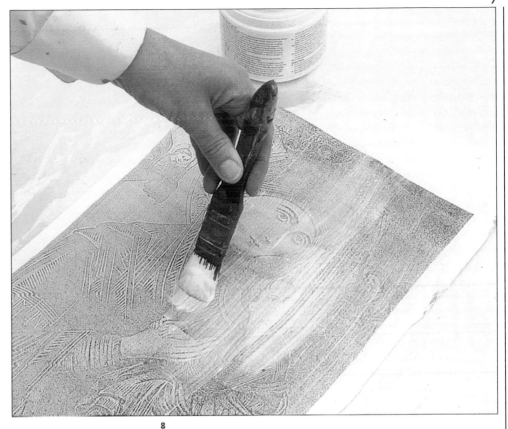

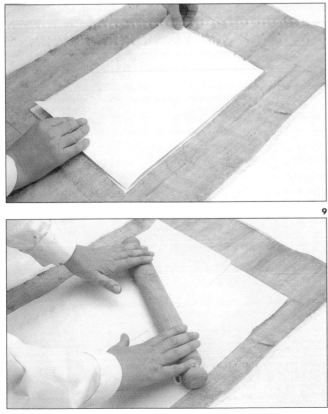

8 As soon as you have finished coating the photocopy with the Image Maker medium, pick it up carefully and position it, image side down, in the middle of the silk, taking care that it is lined up properly with the edges of the gold border. Wash the brush immediately in water.

9 Cover the photocopy with kitchen towel and, using a rolling pin (kept only for craft use) roll evenly over the whole surface in alternate directions for one minute. Remove the kitchen paper without disturbing the photocopy, which should now be adhering to the silk. Leave to dry for approximately 2-3 hours. If you want the image to transfer perfectly then follow the manufacturers' instructions and allow to dry overnight.

10

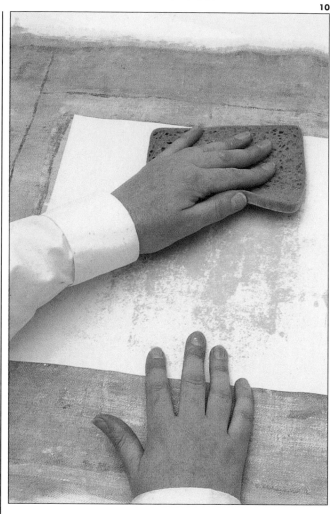

10 With a damp sponge start to moisten the paper backing of the photocopy. Start in the middle and work outwards. The paper will look white at first, but gradually darken as it absorbs the water from the sponge.

11 When the paper is thoroughly dampened, start rubbing it with your finger, beginning in the middle. If the paper is difficult to rub off then dampen a little more with the sponge and wait to allow the water to be absorbed.

11

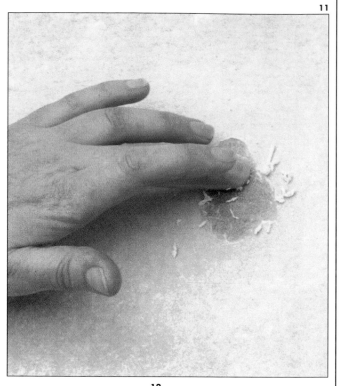

12

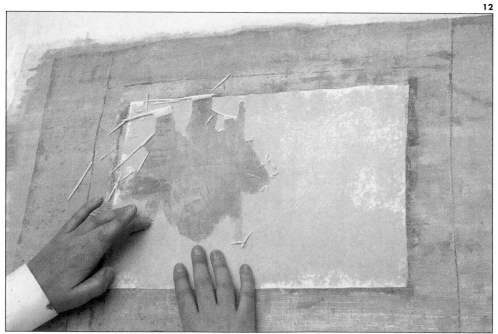

12 As you continue, you will find that you can rub the paper until it rolls up, enabling you to remove it in long pieces.

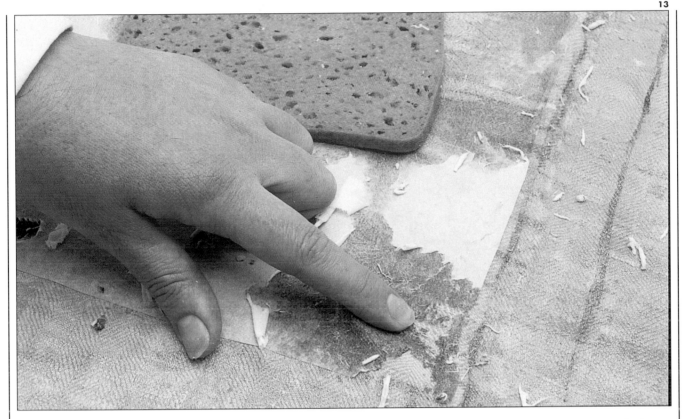

13 Because the Image Maker medium has not been left to dry thoroughly (see step 9), and particularly where it has been painted thinly (see step 7), it is possible to rub and peel off the transferred image in places to give a worn look to the image emerging on the silk. Keep dampening the paper and rubbing with a sponge until all the paper backing looks as though it is removed, and some of the image is removed, too.

14 When the image is thoroughly dry, you will almost certainly see that some of the paper backing has still to be removed. It will appear white and fuzzy on the surface of the image.

15 Start dampening the image with the sponge again, rubbing until the final traces of paper are all removed. Leave to dry.

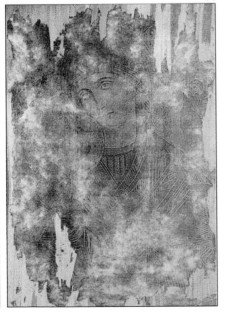

14

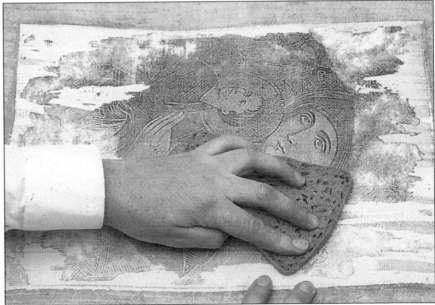

15

16 Using ready-to-use
pigments – Javana colour for
silk, Cherry (8194), Lapis Blue
(8195), Intense Sun Yellow
(8122), Brown (8107) – use an
eye dropper to transfer the
colours and water into a palette
with small containers. Using a
soft no. 3 brush begin to tint
the image with very diluted
colours. If they appear too
bright when you first paint
them you can blot them with
kitchen paper.

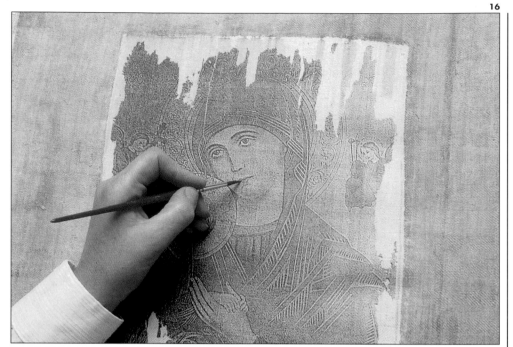

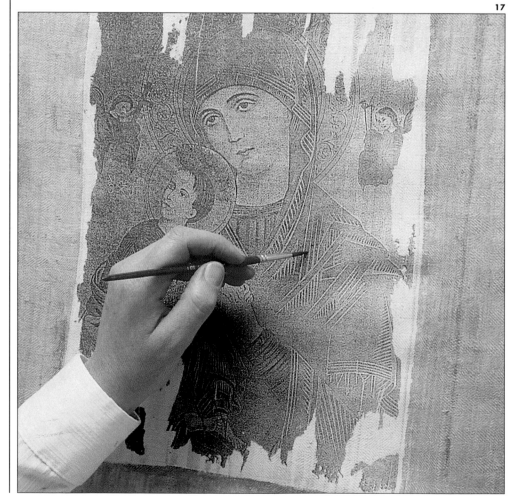

17

17 Build up the darker colours
in layers, using less water in
the dilution. When all the
tinting is dry, fix with a
hairdryer. You should not iron
directly on to the surface of the
transferred image. However,
because the image has been
transferred on to a relatively
thick fabric, it is possible to
iron on the reverse side for
presentation.

18 The herring-bone silk gives a unique quality to this piece. In choosing the reference pictures and deciding which silk to use, then making imaginative use of the transfer method and other media, you will see that every element, however simple, contributes to the final piece. This approach will perhaps inspire you to use your own photographs combined with painting to develop ideas, either for figurative subjects or abstract, textural pieces.

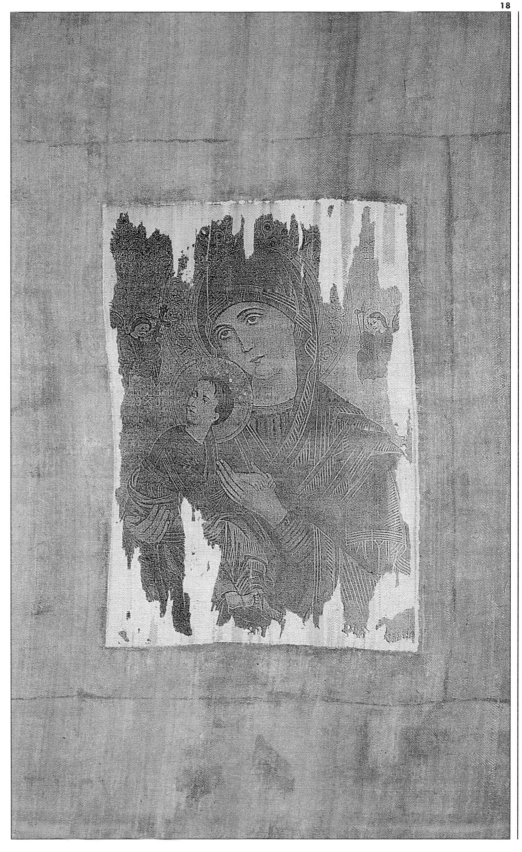

Red Pompeian Panel

PAINTERLY EFFECTS

This project was inspired by a fragment from excavations at Boscoreale near Pompeii. Unlike the project based on the wall-painting with the black background, from Boscotrecase, in Chapter 6, these fragments show that the original paintings at Boscoreale were brightly coloured as well as being rich in architectural and figurative detail. Even though this wall was probably painted around the first century B.C. it retains strong, glowing colours. These colours, in conjunction with the texture of the wall where the surface and paint have been worn away, were the main inspiration for the project.

Silk noile was used, as in the black 'Pompeian' project, for its slightly rough, stone-like surface, and for the way it absorbs colour so well. Noile looks a little like calico, but when painted with dye – as the background is here – the colours take on a glow quite unlike that achieved when painting with dye on other fabrics.

Masking tape is used to lay out the simple, geometric dyed background. Then, after fixing the background with

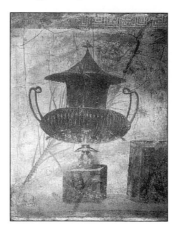

steam, the figurative details are over-painted with Helizarin colour mixed with binder, and opaque white mixed with Helizarin colour. The colour mixed with opaque white visibly sits on the surface of the dyed background, while the colour mixed with binder blends more into the dyed colour. Each, though, picks up and emphasizes the rough surface of the noile.

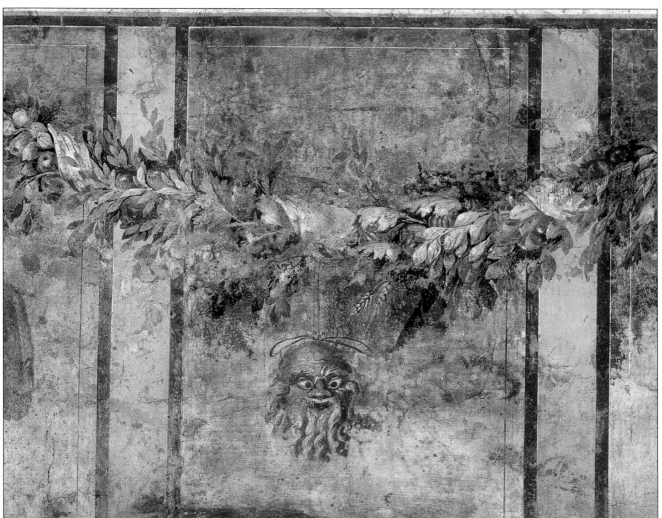

1 Stretch a piece of noile 30x24 in. (76x61cm) on to a previously padded board measuring not less than 34x28 in. (86.5x71cm) (see page 32). Wearing rubber gloves and using a soft, flat 2½ in. (6cm) brush, and clear gutta, paint the background of the silk roughly and lightly, skimming over the surface, leaving plenty of the silk showing through the brush strokes. The aim is to imitate the broken surface of the wall-painting by providing a textured resist to the dye which will be painted next. Do not attempt to cover the silk completely. Leave to dry thoroughly.

2 Mask the sides of the silk, making sure that the tape is straight with an unbroken edge. On the right-hand vertical side, lay down a strip of 2 in. (5cm) masking tape approximately 1in. (2.5cm) inside the masked edge and parallel with it. Repeat on the left-hand side. (See step 6: the masking tape you put down at this point should be in the same position as the yellow vertical stripes shown there.)

Pour some Dupont Rubis (2005) into an enamel dish. Into another enamel dish pour some Manutex F (mixed following the instructions on page 43). Using a 2½ in. (6cm) soft, flat brush, first dip the brush into the Manutex mixture and then into the dye. Paint the dye over the silk quickly and roughly, leaving some of the silk exposed by the brush strokes, alternately dipping the brush into the Manutex and dye as you work. When you have finished painting the red, move on to step 4 and sprinkle the wet red dye with effect salt (Deka Effektsalz is used here). This draws the colour as it dries, giving a mottled effect which becomes more apparent after the piece has been fixed by steaming. Leave to dry and then remove the salt. Return to step 3.

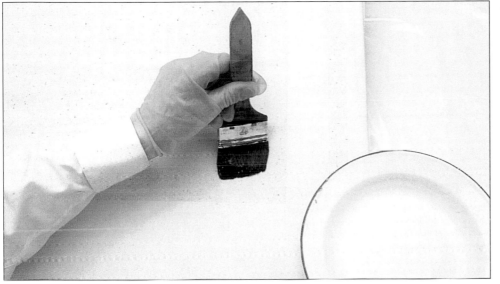

1

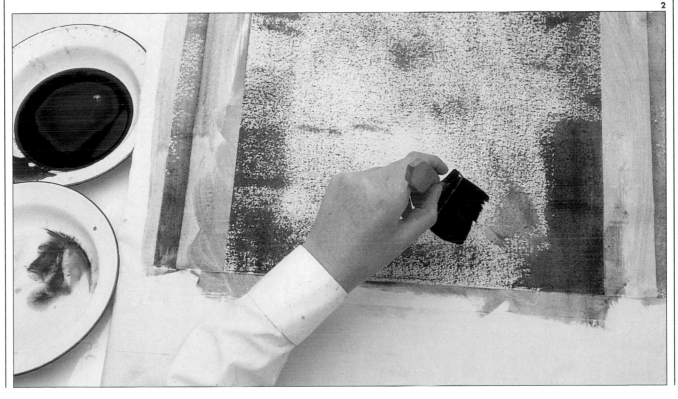

2

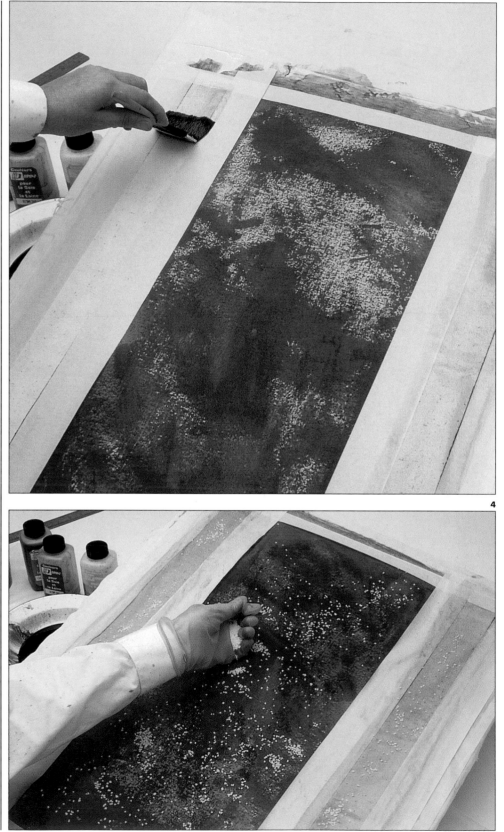

3 Take up the masking tape and discard. This should reveal a vertical 2 in. (5cm) stripe of clean silk on either side. Mask the edges of the two stripes (at the head and foot as well as at the sides). Using Dupont Jaune de Chrome (2000), diluted with water in an enamel dish, and Manutex F alternately on the brush, paint the stripes yellow, again using rough brush strokes. Work a little of the yellow dye into the red background as well.

4 Sprinkle the wet dye with effect salt and leave to dry thoroughly.

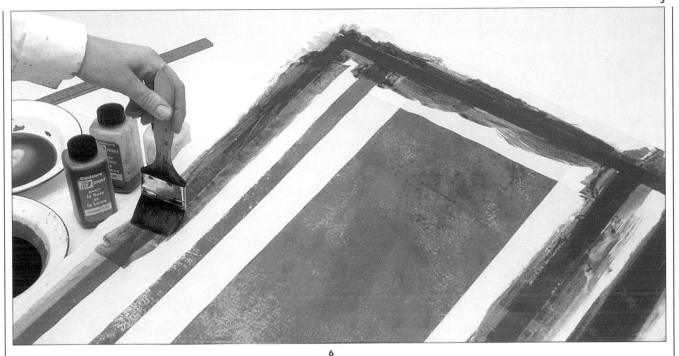

5 Remove the masking tape and discard. Make sure that the yellow stripes are completely dry and cover them with 2 in. (5cm) masking tape, trimming 1 in. (2.5cm) off at the head and foot neatly with scissors. Leaving a 1 in. (2.5cm) gap, lay 2 in. (5cm) tape to the left of the masked stripe, parallel with it, and trim off 1 in. (2.5cm) at the head and foot. Repeat symmetrically on the left-hand side. Mask off the head and foot horizontally, leaving a 1 in. (2.5cm) gap, parallel with the edge, and ensuring that you trim the tape where it overlaps the verticals you have made. Mix a tiny amount of Dupont Canard (2009) and Noir Concentré (2019) into Rubis (2005) on an enamel dish. Mix some Manutex F into this so that it is quite thick and sticky, but still workable with a brush. Using the 2½ in. (6cm) flat, soft brush, roughly paint in the border you have created in the gaps between the masking tape. Leave to dry completely. The Manutex will make the silk feel quite stiff when dry.

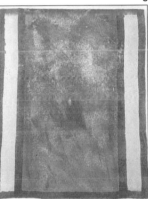

6 Steam, following the instructions on page 48, to fix. Rinse in cold water; wash very thoroughly in warm soapy water to remove all traces of Manutex. Rinse until the water is clear; dry, and iron on the wrong side. If you have washed out the Manutex thoroughly then the silk will once again feel soft and pliable. Do not be alarmed if quite a lot of colour appears to come out during washing; this is not unusual with dark-coloured dyes. Re-stretch on the board; the whole effect of the colour on the silk is now generally softer and the texture made by the combination of gutta resist, rough brush strokes and effect salt shows up much more clearly.

7 Using tailor's chalk, roughly sketch in the position of the garland and the shape of the vase.

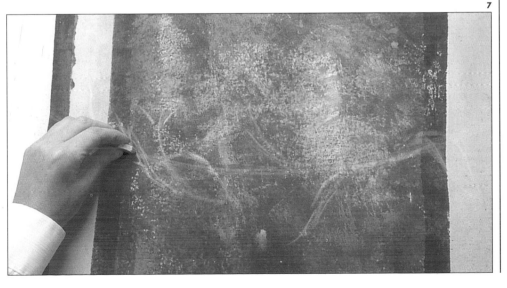

8 Mix Helizarin Red BT into Bricoprint Binder SF20 to make a bright scarlet (full instructions on page 42).

9 Then add Helizarin Blue RT, a little at a time, until a rich ox-blood colour is achieved.

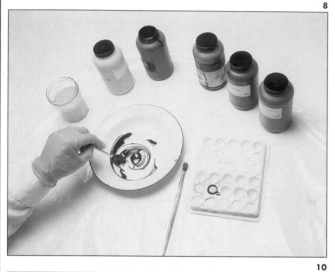

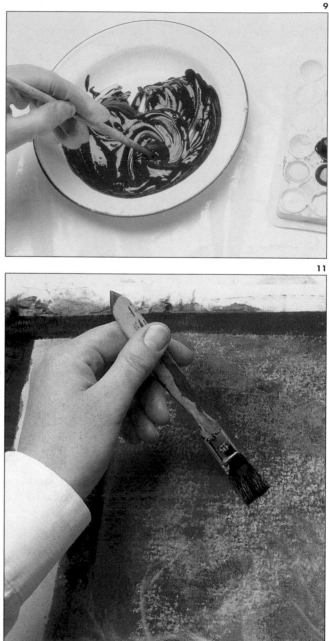

10 Repeat the masking process at step 5 and then overpaint the red border with the Helizarin ox-blood mixture using a ½in. (1.5cm) soft, flat brush and uneven brush strokes, following the direction of the lines.

11 Using the same colour and brush, lightly and roughly add a little overpainting to the background, particularly in the corners. Leave to dry, then remove the masking tape and discard.

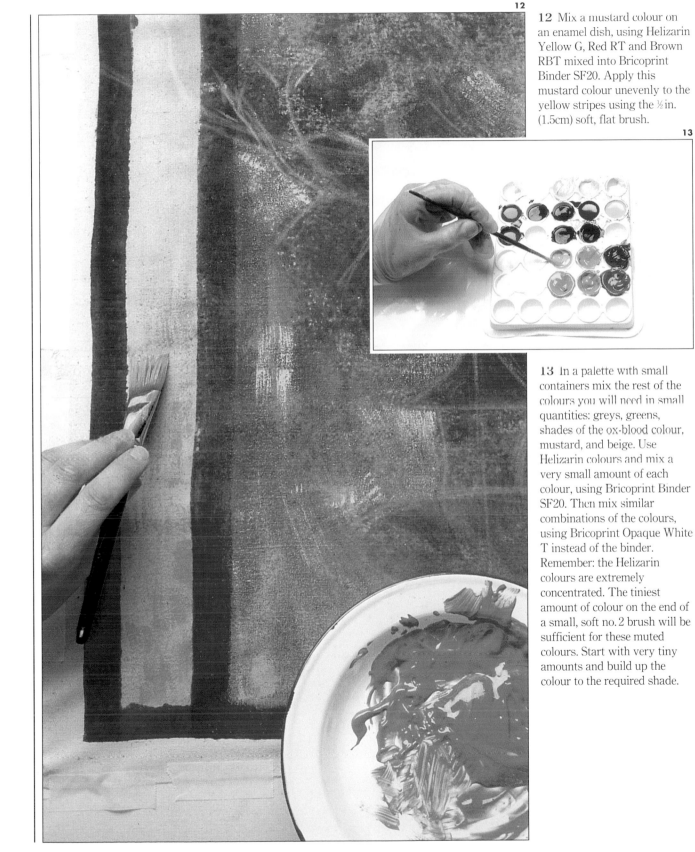

12 Mix a mustard colour on an enamel dish, using Helizarin Yellow G, Red RT and Brown RBT mixed into Bricoprint Binder SF20. Apply this mustard colour unevenly to the yellow stripes using the ½ in. (1.5cm) soft, flat brush.

13 In a palette with small containers mix the rest of the colours you will need in small quantities: greys, greens, shades of the ox-blood colour, mustard, and beige. Use Helizarin colours and mix a very small amount of each colour, using Bricoprint Binder SF20. Then mix similar combinations of the colours, using Bricoprint Opaque White T instead of the binder. Remember: the Helizarin colours are extremely concentrated. The tiniest amount of colour on the end of a small, soft no. 2 brush will be sufficient for these muted colours. Start with very tiny amounts and build up the colour to the required shade.

19 You can now start to paint in the clusters of fruit. These are quite easy to paint because of the depth you have already given to the background with the dye. Use a soft, no. 6 brush and the colours mixed with binder as well as the colours mixed with opaque white. Where the fruit falls on the yellow background allow the yellow to show through your overpainting as highlights. Concentrate on using shades of the ox-blood colour. Where the fruit falls on the red background use shades of the ox-blood colour again (the darkest shade for the outline). Use light brush strokes so that the background shows through the overpainting. Finally, apply the highlights, using the lightest colours mixed into opaque white.

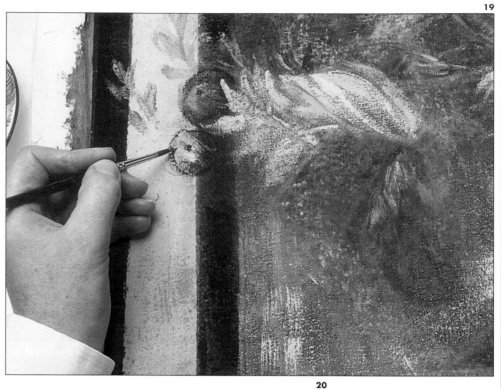

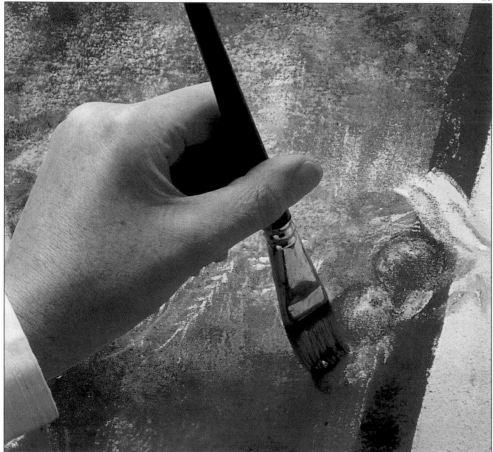

20 Use a large flat, soft 1in. (2.5cm) brush to make the larger leaf shapes, so that the overall effect remains light and rhythmic.

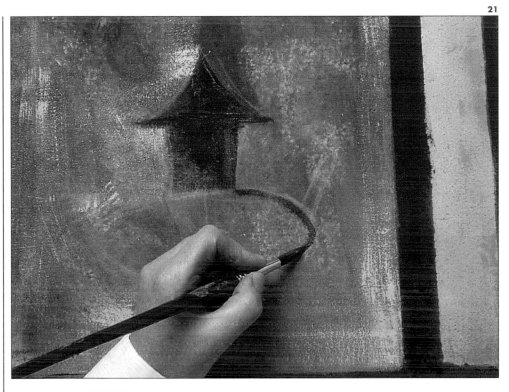

21 When most of the main parts of the garland have been painted in, you can start to paint the vase. Compared with the garland, which is quite complicated to work out and paint, the vase can be painted extremely rapidly. Because the background suggests volume once the outlines are painted, it only requires a few economical lines in the ox-blood colour used for overpainting the border. First sketch out the rough shape of the vase with dark outlines, using light brush strokes.

22 Now you can lightly add the shading. Only a very little of the ox-blood colour is needed, painted sparingly in the darker areas to allow the background tones to show through.

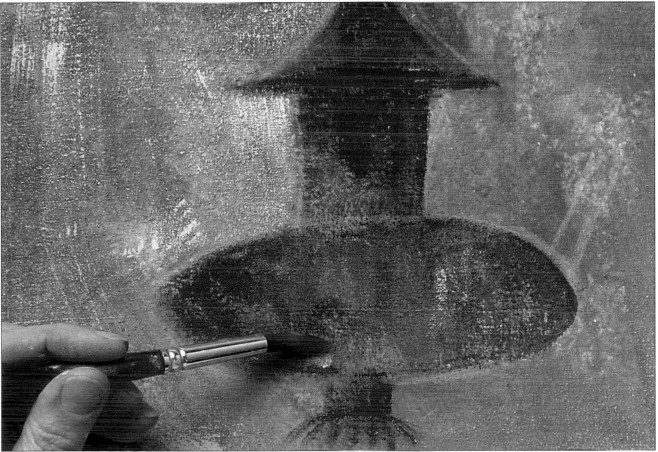

23

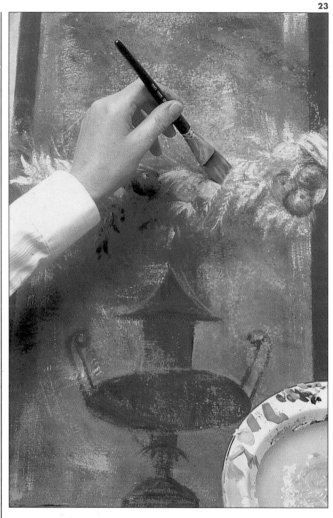

23 When the vase is finished, return to the garland and highlight or darken the background around it to balance the composition in relation to the painted vase.

24 Further surface, chalky texture can be added when the whole piece is dry by lightly applying white wax textile crayon, using the flat side. The marks should be very light, so they just catch on the surface texture of the noile. Finally iron for five minutes on the wrong side, on the cotton setting, to fix.

25 It is possible, when using dyes for backgrounds and pigments for overpainting, to create multi-layered effects. By combining rich, intense colours with the texture of the silk and then employing pigments – either to blend in with the background (Helizarin colour and binder) or to sit on the surface and obscure it to some extent (Helizarin colour and opaque white) – many illusions and effects can be created which are unique to painting on silk. The way you use these effects will ultimately depend on the original reference material from which you choose to work and how you think your ideas can best be conveyed with the available media.

The projects in this book have been taken from mainly decorative reference and have been developed to provide a guide to using the three media on their own, or in combination, to give quite formal results.

It is possible to transfer virtually any mark or image on to silk. Working with the step-by-step instructions supplied here, you should now feel ready to leave formal projects behind and develop your own ideas.

If you do not already keep some kind of notebook of things which inspire you, then now is the time to start. Inspiration for painting on silk can be found everywhere. It might be in the colour of the sky, or an old brick wall; it might be in flowers in the garden or park, or on an old, tattered advertisement hoarding; it might be something you have seen when travelling abroad.

Always be on the look-out for new, visually exciting subjects. By following the projects in this book you should have gained quite a lot of practical experience, even if you might not always have been satisfied with the results! Sometimes making mistakes and then finding ways to correct them can be more useful in terms of development than getting everything right first time. With the information here as your technical guide, you should be ready to develop ideas of your own, both about the imagery you use and the methods you employ.

24

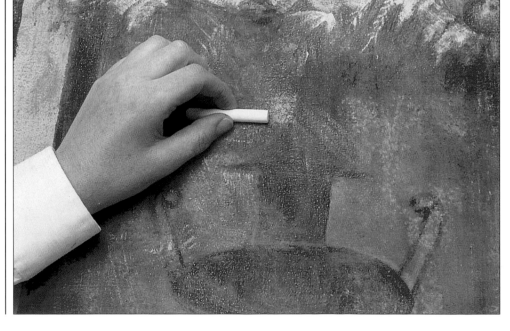

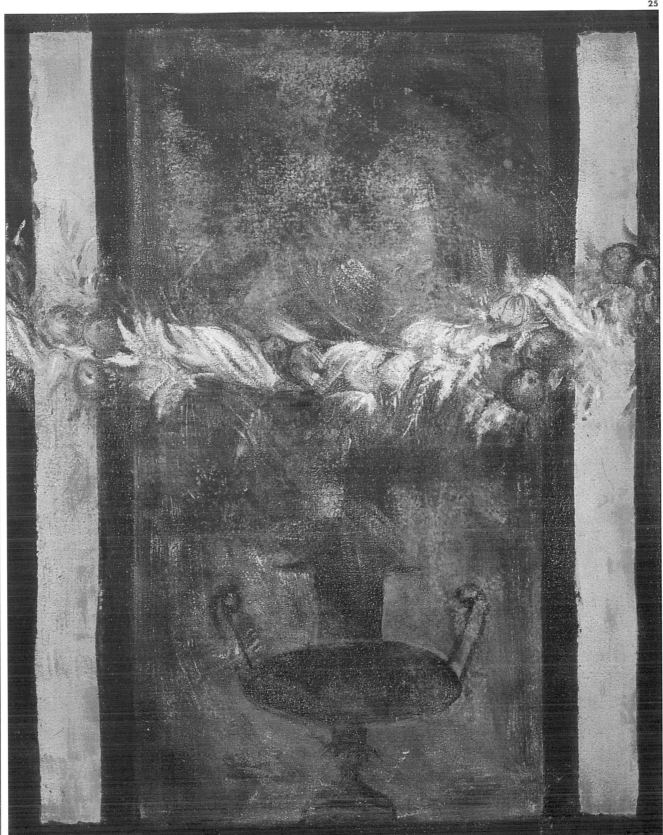

Glossary

Blonde
Natural colour of undyed silk. The term for early 19th-century laces of undyed silk.

Bombyx mori
The domesticated silk moth which is the source of most of the world's silk production.

Chiffon
Transparent silk woven like fine muslin, with a semi-dull lustre and gauze-like grainy texture. Chiffon, organdie, voile and grenadine are all light, matte fabrics made from fine twisted yarns, spaced out to make the fabric transparent, and are all part of the taffeta group of fabrics.

Denier
Unit of weight equal to about 8.5 troy grains, the measure by which silk yarn was weighed and its fineness estimated in 1839.

Douppion
Double cocoon containing male and female pupae, producing a tangled thread. The resulting yarn and woven cloth have a slubbed, irregular texture.

Ply
Yarn of two or more single strands twisted together.

Raw silk
Silk retaining its natural gum or sericin. Though lusterless, it is in its strongest and most durable state. Dye does not penetrate the gum evenly, and the silk is usually de-gummed by immersion in an alkaline solution.

Reeling
The process of unwinding cocoons to make raw silk.

Sericin
Gummy protein that holds together fibroin filaments in a cocoon, and later in raw silk. It prevents even dyeing and is removed by immersion of the raw silk in an alkaline solution.

Sericulture
Cultivation of mulberries and silkworms to make cocoons.

Shot silk
Fabric woven with different coloured warps and wefts, to give an iridescent sheen.

Slubs
Irregular lumps in threads.

Spinning
Spun silk is yarn composed of shorter or broken filaments that are unsuitable for reeling and so require twisting together in the manner of cotton and wool.

Stifle
To kill the pupa in the cocoon by heat.

Taffeta
One of the terms for fine, plain, silk cloth woven by intertwining a warp and a weft yarn in the simplest way. Taffeta is usally shiny, though not highly reflective as satin weaves; yarn-dyed, very fine-grained, with a dry and rustling feel.

Thread
The filament used for sewing, manufactured as part of the throwing operation, but considered a distinct and separate branch because some additional equipment must be used in manufacture, and great care taken in every operation, especially spooling, to make a smooth, knotless thread.

Throwing
The process between reeling of the long filaments of *Bombyx mori* and weaving. The silk thread is twisted gently in varying degrees either to the left or right. Each twist is called a 'turn', and the greater the number of turns the greater the contraction of the thread.

Tussah *(see Wild silks)*

Twill
Fabric in which the weave gives an effect of diagonal ribs and grooves.

Twisting
The process of turning together two or more filaments to form a twisted yarn.

Warps
Lengthwise yarns in woven fabrics.

Weft
Interlacing yarns in woven fabrics.

Wild silks
Term for both truly wild and the less cultivated species of silk moth. The latter includes Indian tussah.

Yarn
Silk which has been reeled and then thrown or else spun.

Ingredients

Heraldry
Blue Panel:
Unbleached taffeta 27x19 in. (68.5x48cm)
Clear gutta
Black lining paint in tube with nozzle
Black wax crayon for use on textiles
Helizarin colours; Blue RT, Yellow G and Bricoprint
    Binder SF20
    or other opaque textile colours.

Yellow and Red Panel with Blue Border:
White taffeta 27x19 in. (68.5x48cm)
Black lining paint in tube with nozzle
Black wax crayon for use on textiles
Textile watercolour primer (e.g. Javana 'Aquarellgrund')
Ready-to-use pigments with reasonable translucency
    (e.g. Cherry Red 8194, Lapis Blue 8195, Intense Sun
    Yellow 8122 *or* Maize Yellow 8192)

Yellow and Red Panel:
Douppion 27x19 in. (68.5x48cm)
Dye for silk (e.g. Jaune de Chrome 2000, Rubis 2005)
Manutex F *or* ready-to-use thickener for use with dyes

Stained Glass
White taffeta 25x17 in. (63.5x43cm)
Helizarin Black TT and Bricoprint Binder SF20
    or Black lining paint
Dye for silk (e.g. Dupont Jaune de Chrome 2000,
    Rubis 2006, Cote d'Azur 2010, Canard 2009, Noir
    Concentré 2019)

Vase of Flowers
Douppion 18x14 in. (45.5x35.5cm)
Dye for silk (e.g. Dupont Noir Concentré 2019)
Ready-to-use thickener *or* Manutex F
Ready-to-use pigment with reasonable translucency
    (e.g. Javana Silk Paint Lapis Blue 8195, Cherry Red
    8194, Intense Sun Yellow 8122 *or* Maize Yellow 8192)

Fleur-de-Lys
Unbleached taffeta 5x3 ft (1.5x0.9m)
Dye for silk (e.g. Dupont Canard 2009, Cote d'Azur 2010)
Gold stencil creme

Italian Grotesque
Tussah 48x24 in. (122x61cm)
Felt-tip pens for textile use (e.g. Javana Art Marker
    Brown 90608, Black 90618)
White wax crayon for textile use
Bricoprint Opaque White T
    or other opaque white for textiles
Helizarin colours; Yellow G, Red BT, Brown RBT
    or other opaque textile media

Black Pompeian Panel
Noile 36x36 in. (91.5x91.5cm)
Clear gutta
Ready-to-use pigments with reasonable translucency
    (e.g. Javana Silk Paint Turquoise 8113, Bordeaux 8117,
    Intense Sun Yellow 8122, Brown 8107)
Helizarin Black TT and Bricoprint Binder SF20
    or Black lining paint
Bricoprint Opaque White T
    or other opaque white for textiles
Black wax crayon for textile use

Icon
Herringbone silk 30x20 in. (76x51cm)
Clear gutta
Ready-to-use pigment with reasonable translucency
    (e.g. Javana Silk Paint Brown 8107, Cherry Red 8194,
    Intense Sun Yellow 8122, Lapis Blue 8195)
Metallic lining paint (e.g. Javana Light Gold 814750,
    Brown 813350)
Dylon Colorfun Image Maker

Red Pompeian Panel
Noile 30x24 in. (76x61cm)
Clear gutta
Dye for silk (e.g. Dupont Rubis 2005, Jaune de Chrome
    2000, Canard 2009, Noir Concentré 2019)
Helizarin colours; Red BT, Blue RT, Yellow G, Brown RBT
    and Bricoprint Binder SF20
    or other opaque textile media
Bricoprint Opaque White T
    or other opaque white for textiles
White wax crayon for use on textiles
Effect salt (e.g. Deka Effektsalz)
Manutex F *or* ready-to-use thickener for use with dyes

Index

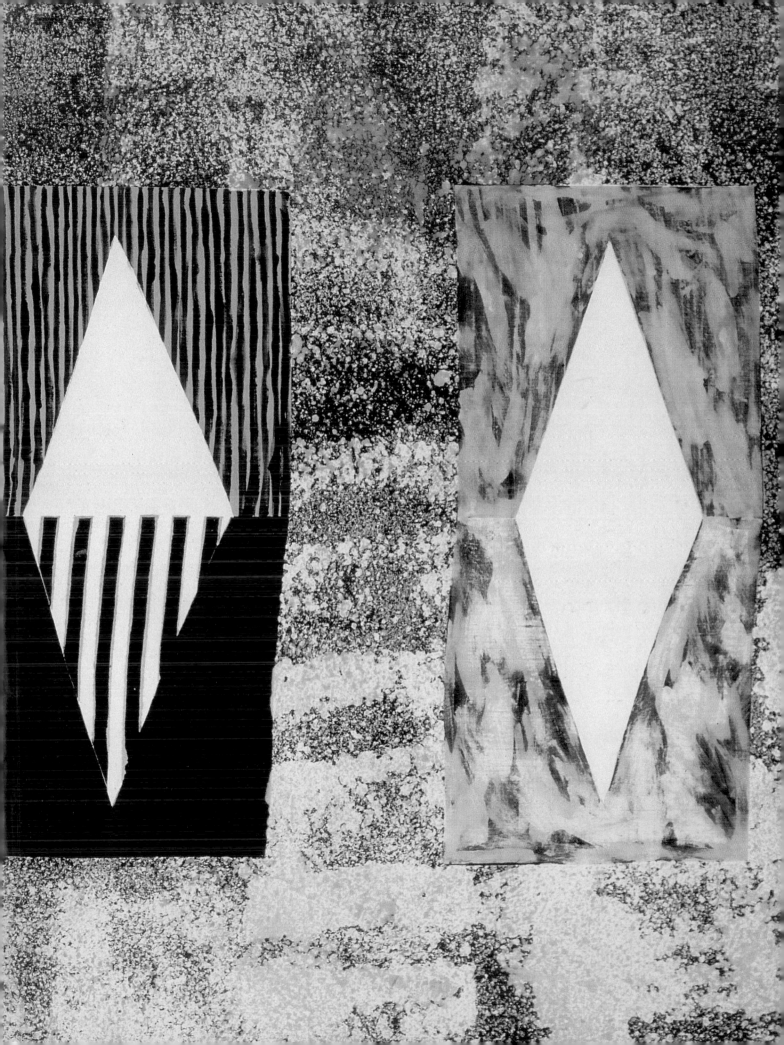